STRANGERS ON A TRAIN

TRUE STRANGE TALES (BOOKS 1-8)

SUSAN SPECHT ORAM

SOS COMMUNICATIONS

Published by SOS Communications LLC in 2025

www.susanspechtoram.com

First Edition

ISBN (paperback): 979-8-9926053-3-4

ISBN (e-book collection): 979-8-9926053-4-1

ISBN (hardcover): 979-8-9926053-5-8

 Formatted with Vellum

GREEN LIGHT

TRUE STRANGE TALES

1

UNEXPECTED ROOMMATE

I was attending a medical conference in Chicago some years back as head of Corporate Communications and Investor Relations for a Seattle biotechnology company. When I checked in at the hotel by the river, a woman at the front desk confirmed my reservation and handed me a key. Just to be sure, I said, "This is a non-smoking room, isn't it?"

The woman frowned, checking her computer screen. "No, it is a smoking room."

"I asked for non-smoking."

She looked up, gazing into my eyes. "Your roommate requested a smoking room. We can't change that."

My jaw dropped. "I don't have a roommate."

She nodded. "Yes, you do. It's a double bed room. You have the same confirmation number."

My eyebrows shot up. "Who is it?"

"Dr. Agarwal."

"But I don't know him. I've never met him. How could this happen?" I pulled out my hotel confirmation number and showed it to her.

She shrugged. "That's the same confirmation code we have for the two of you."

"But there's been a mistake. I need a different room. I can't share with him."

She looked at me like I was being difficult, and she'd had a busy, trying day. "I'm sorry, but the hotel is fully booked, and we can't change your reservation."

"The computer must have made a mistake. Please, find me another room. I'll sleep in the basement if I have to."

She shook her head, looking past me to the next person in line, and I stood my ground, narrowing my eyes. I didn't want to share my room with a stranger, even if he was well-regarded in oncology circles. I'd read his articles in scientific journals.

The idea of being forced to have an unexpected roommate made my jaw tense, and I marched away, determined not to share a room. I went up to two people I worked with who were staying at the same swanky hotel.

Leni's eyes opened wide. "Dr. Agarwal is your roommate? He's really well-known."

Another woman nodded. "He's giving a presentation at this conference. I'm going to hear him speak."

I swallowed hard, because my secret roommate was a

hit with everyone but me. They were impressed and acted as if it might be a boon for me.

A woman joked, "Keep the room, get to know him better."

I half-smiled. "He's a smoker. And I've got Jerry at home anyway."

Eventually, a friend who was in charge of an event at the hotel appealed to her contact, and the hotel found me a hotel room in the basement down a dim hallway. I was content in a room to myself, until the next strange hotel episode took place.

2

YOU ALREADY CHECKED IN

I stood in line and finally got to the front counter at a major hotel in New York City. "I'm checking in, Susan Specht."

A young woman in her mid-twenties tapped away on a keyboard and frowned. Seconds passed. She asked for my hotel confirmation number, which I provided.

I held my breath. Not again. A mistake couldn't happen a second time. Everyone else in my group checked in and left for their rooms,

She glanced up, holding my gaze, "You already checked in, so we gave your second room away. I don't know why there were two reservations. It was a mistake."

I blinked, standing at the check-in counter at night after flying in from Seattle. We had a big event tomorrow with investors, and I needed to sleep.

"I'm sorry, what did you say? I had two rooms? And you cancelled one?"

She nodded. "Yes, you had two reservations, and when you checked in this afternoon, we canceled the other one."

I showed her my hotel reservation confirmation number, but she shrugged.

I said, "I didn't check in earlier today, because I was flying from Seattle. There must be another person with my name staying in this hotel."

She shook her head. "That's very unlikely."

"Would you please check? Who is the other person who has my name?"

She tapped at the keyboard. "Are you Susan Specht from Rhode Island?"

"No, I'm Susan Specht from Seattle. There's been a mistake, and I need a room."

She pursed her lips. "Can I see some identification?"

I showed her my driver's license, and she squinted at it. "We don't have anything available. The hotel is fully booked."

I suppressed a groan. I needed to get a bed, not with the other Susan Specht, but all by myself. "Please," I said, "please find me somewhere to sleep here tonight and soon. I've had a long day. I'll take anything you have."

I ended up in a smoking room right by a chiming elevator that came and went all night. But it didn't matter, because I could close the door and sit on the bed all by myself. Perhaps my secret roommate, assigned by a Chicago hotel computer, would have enjoyed it. But I didn't invite him.

3

THE ENGINEERS

I was in New York City another time for business meetings, staying on a hotel near Times Square. I walked in, locked the door and slid a chain across for security. When I opened my suitcase, someone used a key card outside and turned the door knob.

My heart thudded, and I strode to the door. "This room is taken. Go away."

The key card clicked a second time, and the door slowly opened, but I held a foot against the door, and a chain across the opening kept the stranger from entering.

I slammed the door shut with my hip. "Go away. I'll call security."

Hearing male voices speaking in low tones on the other side of the door, I peered out through the peephole at two middle-aged men in green coveralls with ball caps pulled down over their eyes. A lean man on the other side of the door said in a gruff voice, "Engineering. Let us in." A shorter man nodded and put his hands on his hips.

"Go away."

The skinny, taller man pushed a key card in the slot on his side of the door again. The door clicked open, but I pushed back. My hands were sweating. My knees were trembling.

"Engineering."

In a trembling voice, I said, "I don't think so. Go away."

The men spoke to each other, and the stout one leaned in, saying, "We're here to fix your TV."

"I didn't call for that. Nothing's wrong with the TV. Go away."

They murmured to each other and shuffled away, heads down.

I whooshed out a breath and called the front desk, saying what had happened.

A man said in a concerned voice, "They weren't our staff. We'll look into this."

4

CHIPPED TOOTH

In elementary school, I played flute in band and during a school concert, I stood with Janet and Sally. Rehearsal had gone well, but when I gazed at the assembled students and teachers, my hands went cold. The music teacher started playing the piano and the audience stared at us.

Janet and Sally started to play. My face heated with a blazing fire of embarrassment. I grasped the cold nickel flute with trembling hands. My body broke out in a sweat.

I blew into the flute, but no sound came out. I tried to join in, but in my head, I was wallowing in a lake of self-doubt and shyness.

My lower lip was moist with sweat. The flute slipped off my mouth. I held the instrument and managed to get two notes out of it at the end of the piece. People in the audience clapped. Sally and Janet gave me doubtful looks, and our music teacher later said, "I thought three flutes were supposed to be playing, but I only heard two."

I think the problem was, my body matured early. I developed breasts and wore a bra in fourth grade. Boys chased me during recess, trying to snap my bra, while I ran away. Teachers on duty glanced over and did nothing. I never told my parents about the bullying. I was ashamed about my body being different from other girls.

One day, things got out of hand. Alan chased me, calling me names. "Broad girl, broad girl, I'm going to get you."

"BG," yelled another boy, coming after me.

I fled for the far side of the fenced school yard, near where my teacher was standing smoking a cigarette and talking with another teacher. Randy ran after me, and Gordon went around a jungle gym before advancing on me.

They closed in on me, and I was trapped, standing by a metal circle in a play structure. Alan, who has now passed away, I noticed in the obits, shoved my head inside the metal circle and before I could react, he karate chopped my neck, the force of the side of his hand drove my head down hard. My front tooth met metal with a mighty crack.

I cried out, and the boys vanished. My neck hurt, and I rubbed it. I ran my tongue around my mouth. Part of my front tooth was gone. I started to cry, standing there in the playground at recess in the fourth grade. Two teachers strode over and asked what was happening.

"Part of my tooth is missing. He karate chopped me."

I was sent to the school principal, who sat me down and glared, as if the incident was my fault. I explained what happened, and he stood up. "I suppose," he said with a heavy sigh, "we should go look for the rest of your tooth."

We hunted around in dirt and debris, but we didn't find the end of my front tooth. My parents never talked to me about it, that I recall. My mother took me to a dentist, who said, "The tooth might grow in. I recommend we leave it and see what happens."

You might guess my experiences of being bullied in grade school made me a cheerleader for underdogs in my books, and you're right. You can see my chipped front tooth in author chats on my YouTube channel (Susan Specht Oram Author).

5

CHECK BETWEEN HER TOES

My girl-boy twins were in seventh grade when I got a call from the middle school counselor. "Two parents called me to say your daughter is dealing drugs at school. Their children told them about it."

My daughter was home with a fever, and I'd taken the day off work to be with her. I screw up my face and said, "What exactly did they say?"

"That she's shooting up heroin in the boy's locker room during school, and she's selling drugs."

I shook my head. "I seriously doubt that."

My red-headed daughter had been a target for bullying, despite my efforts, since Montessori preschool, where three girls pushed her down in the bathroom. I arrived to pick up my kids at preschool, but the door to my daughter's classroom was closed. They were having a special meeting.

I leaned against the wall, wondering what the problem was and talked with another mother. The door opened and four and five-year old students shuffled out. The teacher called me in and said my daughter had been pushed down in the bathroom, and the school had a no tolerance for behavior like that. It never happened again, and my daughter doesn't remember the incident, but it shows how cruel little humans can be.

The middle school counsellor spoke, bringing me back to the present. "She's home sick today, is that right?"

"Yes, she has a fever, and she's sleeping right now."

"I want you to go and check her for needle marks."

"What?"

"Yes, check between her fingers and toes and on her legs and arms for where she might have shot up."

I whooshed out a breath. "This is nuts, but I'll do it. Who started these rumors?"

"I'll hold on while you look.'

I let out a sigh, set down the phone and slipped into my daughter's bedroom, where she was fast asleep in bed, cheeks flushed red. I gently examined her, looking between her toes and her fingers, on her legs and arms. Her eyelids fluttered, but she didn't wake up.

I slipped out of the room and closed the door. Picking up the phone, I said in a low voice, "There's nothing there.

No punctures or needle marks. Nothing. These accusations are absurd. She's in seventh grade, for heaven's sake."

"I'm sorry but I had to ask you to do that because two parents called about it and another mother told the principal."

I groaned. "Who is spreading these rumors? Do you know?"

"I don't know, but I'll try to find out. We may never know."

"This is crazy. A kid shooting up heroin in the boy's locker room? And parents believed it?"

"They did and they want your daughter kicked out of school for it."

"She's being targeted because she's different, with her curly red hair and telling people she's gay."

"And the hooded black cape she wears doesn't help but attract attention."

"She wanted the cape, and I helped her sew it. It was her idea."

"Well, it makes her stand out."

"No one should be accused of dealing drugs when they're not doing it. Please, get to the bottom of this rumor and squash it like a bug."

"I'll try. I'll call students into my office and try to pry it out of them."

The counsellor chased the rumor, which wafted through school like a wispy cloud you can't catch in your hands. She called me a week later to report she hadn't gotten to the bottom of it.

I said, "A girl was friends with my daughter until recently, and there was a rift. Maybe she started the rumor."

"I'll check. But I want you to know, parents are still complaining about your daughter being in school. I believe you, that she's not dealing drugs."

A week later, she called. "You may be right. The rumor might have come from that other girl, but I can't pin it down or get her to confess. We'll consider the matter closed, and I'll tell the parents who reported this to let it go."

6

WHIPS ON THE WALL

I met a young woman in her twenties at a biotechnology company. Jane was an administrative assistant and when she left for another job, I was offered her position. Months later, Jane invited me to lunch at her Pike Place Market apartment. I didn't know her well, but I went out of curiosity.

I took the elevator up, and Jane welcomed me into an elegant apartment with white leather furniture. She watched as I paused in front of a featured wall, decorated with black leather whips and handcuffs.

I shrugged, because I'd worked as an artist and sold work in galleries and at art fairs for ten years. I figured the display must be someone's idea of art.

Jane smiled, which she rarely did when we worked together for a short time. I had pegged her as a nervous type who preferred PowerPoint slide shows to talking with people. We sat outside on her balcony, munching on take-out salads and making small talk. We had little in common and the dull conversation confirmed it. She was single and ten years younger than me. My twins were about to enter middle school.

She set down her fork and faced me, ignoring the shimmering water of Elliott Bay and a ferry departing the dock. "Have you ever thought about becoming a dominatrix?"

My fork hung in midair. My eyebrows slid up, and my jaw dropped.

She tilted her head and continued talking as if we knew each other well and were friends who could bare our souls, sharing intimate details. She gestured to the apartment, which was well-appointed in a sought-after location near the waterfront. "I don't just work as an administrative assistant for an insurance company now, I also work nights and on weekends as a dominatrix."

I swallowed and listened, curious about her double life.

She grinned. "That's how I pay for all this. I make a lot of money on the side. Guys in tech are willing to pay a lot for a woman to use a whip on them."

I cringed but was spellbound by her secret. With her big round glasses, chubby cheeks and curly brown hair, I never guessed she would crack a whip in the bedroom.

I gulped. "I never knew there was demand for that."

She nodded, leaning in. "I can't handle all the clients

who want to see me. There are too many, and I'd like to hire you to work with me."

"It's not something I've thought of doing."

She tapped a red lacquered fingernail on the black metal patio table. "It's easy to do, and you'll rake it in. We'll take cash and split the proceeds. You can work only one night a week if you want. Just crack the whip in the air, tell them things and boss them around in the bedroom, handcuffing them."

I drew in a slow breath. I needed more money. Child support was overdue, and I was in the process of garnishing my ex's wages. My kids thought I like eating scrambled eggs for dinner, but really that was what I could afford.

I wanted to let her down gently, but questions cawed in my mind, like pesky crows perched on my shoulder. This was my one chance to gather snippets of strange information from a reliable source. I said, "Isn't it risky?"

She shrugged. "I've had no problem so far. And the money I'm making is unbelievable."

I crossed my arms. I was due back at work in ten minutes. "How do people find you?"

"Craig's list and personal ads in the paper."

I let out a long sigh. "I appreciate the offer, but I'm not interested."

She beamed. "You'd be great. They'd love you."

"Sorry, it's not my thing." I stood and thanked her for lunch.

She walked me to the door, and I glanced at the wall featuring crisscrossed whips and handcuffs with a new understanding of what it meant. Opening the door for me, she smiled. "Think about it and get back to me if you change your mind. We'd be partners, and I'd keep you busy. You'd make an unbelievable amount of money."

The door closed behind me, and I rode the elevator down, realizing everyone carries secrets and I would never have guessed hers. I strode past Pike Place Market and headed to my office job. Sliding into my seat and answering the phone at work, I smiled, because I had another story to tell.

7

ROLLING PIN

The door to my pottery studio flung open. Window panes and pottery vases and bowls on glass shelves rattled. A man in his early twenties stood in my shop, eyes darting around. Sensing danger, I clutched a huge, heavy rolling pin at a table in back, where I was rolling out clay to form platters.

He lurched forward, frantic and frenetic, extending his hands, looking ready to grab cash and run. Sweat beaded on his brow. I glanced at the phone, ten feet away.

His gaze slid over a cookie tin, where I stored cash and checks until the end of the day. His eyes latched onto a door leading to a bathroom, and a side door, blocked by my larger kiln.

He stopped and blinked, slack mouth hanging open, and I raised my rolling pin in the air, saying in a firm voice, "You'd better leave before I call the cops."

He turned and fled, pots quaking in his wake. I locked the door, turned the open sign to closed, and returned to work, slicing slabs of clay with a sharp needle tool. And that was the last I saw of him or anyone like that.

8

THE CUSTOMERS' SON

An older couple, and I thought they were ancient then, being as how I was younger, so maybe they were in their early fifties, came in my pottery studio one afternoon. I didn't have kids yet, but I observed how careful the parents were, their bodies reacting to every twitch and jerky gesture from their maybe thirty-year-old son.

They looked around and spoke with me, and their son tried to speak, but I couldn't understand him, so I think I said something about why I made pottery and pointed to my two kilns, where the pots were fired. The son nodded to me, and they left, gently closing the door.

Months later, the parents came in without their son. They thanked me for being kind to him before (I mean, of course, who wouldn't?) and told me this story. They'd never taken a vacation since their son was born, because they didn't want to leave him with anyone else. But it was time to try a holiday, and a social worker suggested they try leaving him at a halfway house near the university.

With great trepidation, they dropped off their son, said goodbye and flew off for their first vacation in thirty years. They beamed when they told me what happened while they were away, worrying of course, as parents do, about their child left behind.

A kind woman at the halfway house pointed to a typewriter on a desk and asked their son if he knew how to use it. She showed him how it worked. He wasn't able to form words, but he sat down and typed out a letter to his parents.

A tear trickled down the mother's cheek, and she wiped it away before she told me, "His letter said he appreciated everything we'd done for him for so many years, but he wanted to live on his own. He was ready to move out of our home. He said he loved us and knew we meant well, but he wanted more freedom and to make his way in the world."

She dabbed her eyes with a tissue. Her husband patted her back as they stood in front of my "Sale" table with marked down pottery, intended to draw people in and make them lifetime customers. He said, "We never knew. We didn't know if he could think or what was going on in his mind. All these years, and we never knew."

"Wow, that's a wonderful story," I said with a smile. "I'm glad it worked out like it did."

She nodded. "What if we hadn't taken that trip? We never would have known he wanted his independence."

He shook his head. "What if the typewriter hadn't been there? I had no idea fully formed thoughts were going through his head. He wrote us a letter."

They walked out hand in hand, leaving for the next chapter in their lives.

9

WAKING UP DURING SURGERY

My surgeon, who was a breast cancer survivor, called and said on a Friday evening, "I'm sorry to tell you this, but the pathology results show you have cancer and we didn't get the margins. They double-checked the results to make sure it was right."

My stomach churned, and I gripped my husband's hand.

He blinked back tears, listening to the doctor on speaker phone.

The surgeon said, "You need another surgery to remove the cancer."

My mouth hung open. "But I thought it looked benign?"

"It did, but it is breast cancer, and we need to schedule

the surgery right away. Call the office on Monday to set it up."

We hung up, and I burst into tears, weeping on a man's shoulder who was familiar with death, dying and disease. His mother was diagnosed with multiple sclerosis when he was young and she passed away from cancer when he was seventeen. He helped her around the house, she taught him to cook meals, and he knew the long grind we were about to face. But to his credit, he didn't tell me that. He let me think the second and third surgeries would be easy, which is what I needed.

I went in for surgery, trying to be optimistic, and watched a young man stride around the pre-op room. He was shorter than the other workers, and he held his head high when he walked. He had a brisk stride, while others glided around, as if conserving energy for a long day ahead.

He came over to my bed and said he'd be my anesthesiologist. He left and my surgeon stopped by, cheeks glowing under a blue surgery hair bonnet. She patted my arm and left, and I sighed, knowing I was in good hands with her. But little did I know what awaited me in the operating room.

They wheeled me in, and I looked up at bright operating room lights. Hospital employees buzzed about, garbed in blue gowns, wearing face masks over their noses and mouths. The anesthesiologist put a mask over my face, told me to breathe in and count to ten, and I did, closing my eyes and drifting off.

Awareness crept in, and I heard my surgeon talk about a female who was sick with pancreatitis. It sounded like she was talking about a dog. I wondered if I was dreaming, but the conversation continued. Did I have pancreatitis, and they were talking about me?

Instruments clanged in metal bowls. Conversation about the sick female continued. I realized I must be awake during surgery, but I couldn't open my eyes. I tried to talk, but nothing came out of my mouth. Was I having a nightmare? Maybe I was dreaming and imagining this.

On went the conversation. They were operating on my left chest wall, but thank goodness, I didn't feel a thing.

I had to tell them something was wrong. I tried to yell, giving it a tremendous effort, but no words or sounds issued from my mouth. I was awake in a living nightmare, but no one knew. And yet they were right by my side.

Move the hand, I told myself. Wiggle your fingers. You can do it.

I tried to wiggle my right hand, but it was strapped down. Nothing happened. Focusing on my left hand, I told my fingers to move. Wiggle fingers, in the left hand, move.

The operation continued. It was only going to get worse. I had to get their attention. Now.

Putting all my effort into it, concentrating as hard as I

could, I beamed all my force into my left hand's fingers farthest from the thumb. Move. Now. Tell them I'm awake.

"Hand me," my surgeon said. I knew her voice. I was truly awake. I had to get their attention. I moved my left fingers a little, putting all my effort into it.

"I think she's awake," a nurse on my left side said.

No one responded. Conversation continued. Instruments clanged.

I moved my fingers again, giving it all I had. The little finger was most responsive, followed by the one next to it. Those digits saved me.

The nurse said in a high-pitched loud voice, "She moved her fingers. She's awake."

My surgeon said to the person behind my head, "Put her under."

No response came from the anesthesiologist. I wiggled the fingers on my left hand. The operating room grew silent and still. My surgeon boomed in a loud voice, "Put her down. Right now!"

Next thing I knew, I woke up in the recovery room. Blinking my eyes, I watched the anesthesiologist skitter around the room, looking agitated. He came over to me and said, "You didn't wake up during surgery."

I frowned. "I heard the surgeon talking about a sick female. I heard instruments clang. If I wasn't awake, why did she tell you to put me under?"

His face flushed, and he rubbed the back of his neck. "You didn't wake up during surgery."

I croaked, "Yes, I did."

He scuttled away like a water bug being chased by a slithering snake, and if I could have beaned him right there, I would have. What a jerk to gaslight me, especially when I was woozy from surgery. I took a slow breath and tried to calm my racing heart.

My surgeon stopped by. "I'm sorry you went through that."

"I heard you talking about a female with a disease. She had pancreatitis. Were you talking about your dog?"

Her eyes opened wide. "Yes, I was talking about my dog. You heard that?"

"I did. But he didn't believe me." I pointed at the traitor anesthesiologist across the room, who should have kept me asleep on the operating room table.

My doctor leaned over and looked at him, where he was pretending to arrange something but not moving things. He gave us a furtive glance and left.

She nodded to me. "I believe you, and I'll speak with him about this. I was talking about my dog, and you heard it. The nurse saw you move your left hand."

I let out a long sigh and leaned back into the pillow. One of the worst things in life is to not be believed about something you know is true. The next day, my husband wrote a lengthy polite but scathing letter to the hospital CEO telling them what happened and how it must never happen again. My surgeon, when we saw her on my next visit, said it was the best letter the hospital had received and it was sent to department heads and given a great deal of attention. She said the person at fault was being given additional training, and she apologized and promised it would never happen again.

A few years later, I was in a local writing class and read a short fiction piece aloud about the incident. Another student spoke up and said it never happens. She knew because she was married to the chief anesthesiologist at the hospital, who told her patients think they woke up during surgery, but they're wrong.

"You imagined it," she said.

"But it happened," I told her in a stern voice. "My doctor acknowledged it, and I heard her talking about her sick dog. And if it wasn't real, why did my surgeon tell the anesthesiologist to put me under during the operation?"

She fiddled with her papers and shook her head. "It doesn't happen."

I met her chief anesthesiologist husband briefly at a book signing, but his eyes wouldn't meet mine. She bought my first novel, *Shore Lodge*, and they hurried out into a dark, rainy night, probably glad to be free of me, an outlier and prover of things that never happen.

10

A NEW DOG

My husband glanced at a photo of the rescue dog I wanted to adopt. Our beagle-mix rescue dog had passed away five months before, and I figured if we weren't going to travel in retirement, we might as well welcome a new furry member into our family. Jerry said, "She's a homely girl. She looks like Dobbie in the Harry Potter movies."

In her online photo, Abby was gaunt with a haunted look and sad brown eyes. I said, "She needs a home, and she's part beagle like Buddy was. She weighs only twenty-two pounds, so she'll be easy to lift. We can help her."

He sighed. He'd rejected the idea of adopting a cute smiling puppy named Jack the week before. "Okay, let's see if she's available."

Three weeks later, we pulled up on a dark September before dawn morning in a parking lot in Marysville, north of Seattle, by a pet store. A big long truck was already there, having come all the way from Austin, Texas to Idaho, dropping off pets along the way, and to Western Washington before heading south to Oregon. Rain drizzled down, splattering the windshield.

A smiling middle-aged woman in a white hazmat suit stepped out of the bus and hurried over with a clipboard. I said, "We're here to pick up Abby. She's a beagle-mix."

The woman's eyes narrowed when I mentioned beagle-mix, as was listed on the website, and she glanced at her clipboard, clearing her throat. She paused for a beat before saying, "Yes, here she is. I'll bring her out in a few minutes."

We'd seen photos online of the animals journey, where cats in hammocks looked miffed to be in close proximity to dogs. Oddly though, I didn't see any photos of Abby.

The woman went back to the truck. Dogs howled with a gut-wrenching sound. I whispered to Jerry, "I hope she'll be as good as Buddy was."

He said in a gruff voice, because it was early, and we hadn't had coffee yet, "No dog will ever be as good as Buddy was."

I nodded. "Buddy was the best."

So our new girl had big feet to fill, and when she was brought to the front of the truck, her ears were down, and her tail was between her legs. She squatted right there at the entrance inside the truck, letting out a long stream of urine. Abby balked on the leash, so the rescue shelter volunteer gathered Abby in her arms and brought her over to where I sat in the back seat with the door open, waiting for our new pup.

She placed Abby in my arms, handed me paperwork and shut the door, waving and walking away. Other dogs left the truck walking on leash to the new owner's cars, but Abby quivered and shook and trembled, quaking in my arms. I cooed to her and sang a little silly song, but the shaking continued.

"She's really upset," I said in a low voice.

Jerry drove and clenched his jaw. "Hope we didn't make a mistake."

Fast forward to being home, where instead of walking on a leash, she melted on the pavement and managed to wrap herself with the leash around a Rhododendron plant. She ran from my husband when he opened his arms in the kitchen and hid under a table.

She cowered and trembled, and the first two nights, she whined to go out, tail between her legs every hour and a half. Being sleep-deprived wasn't something I'd planned on with a one-year-old rescue dog, but we soon learned from a vet that she was more like nine months old.

I also learned that she'd been captured by the dog catcher in a small town in Texas. I looked up the dog catcher online and discovered my husband bore a resemblance to the dog catcher. In fact, Abby didn't like men. This was going to be a problem.

Jerry fed Abby and gave her treats. A month later, her tail popped out from between her legs and we learned when she's happy, her tail curls. It took a few years, but finally, Abby and Jerry are friends, and she leans on him when he sips coffee and reads the news by the fire in the mornings. She didn't turn out to be a beagle-mix at all, but that doesn't matter. She's a love, and that's what we needed, a forty-nine-pound yellow dog who is starting her life over with us.

11

GREEN LIGHT

I sat at the red light, the old sedan engine chugging, with my four-year-old twins in the back, heading to preschool. Rain drummed down and wiper blades groaned. A hush fell over the car.

"Tell us a story," my kids said.

"Not now," I said in a quiet voice, keeping my eyes trained on the busy intersection. We were two cars back.

Out of the clear blue, I hear a man's voice that sounded like my father's say, "Green doesn't always mean go."

My head jerked. This was a first. My eyebrows shot up, and I shook my head to clear the strange moment. It was like someone had spoken into my left ear.

The light ahead turned green at the busy North Seattle intersection. The car in front of us moved forward and drove away, but an invisible force held me back. I kept my right foot frozen in place, poised over the accelerator.

My kids piped up, "Drive, Mom, drive."

The car behind us honked, but I heard the clear voice say a second time, "Green doesn't always mean go." I stayed where I was.

Second later, a flatbed truck raced down the hill to my left, running the red light. It blew through the intersection and rumbled past, carrying a full load of tall propane tanks, and raced west on Holman Road.

I blew out a breath and pushed on the accelerator pedal, driving south. My hands trembled, gripping the steering wheel tight, and my heart thumped.

"Why didn't you go, Mama?"

"Because green doesn't always mean go."

Next up is Book 2, *The Train*, in the *Strangers on a Train Series*.

THE TRAIN

TRUE STRANGE TALES

1

THE TRAIN

I switched long-distance phone carriers often and finally accrued enough frequent flyer miles for a trip to Europe. I booked a flight from Seattle into Paris and out of Rome,

In Paris, I sketched in museums and ate croissants in cafes. I walked all day and took three baths in two days in my hotel room, floating and fighting jet lag.

Taking the night train from Paris to Florence sounded like a good idea. I didn't care about having five strangers for roommates at first. But as I settled into my bunk and fell asleep, a sound woke me up. A little while later, it happened again.

One bunk mate, a woman in her late twenties stepped out of the couchette, slamming the door shut behind her. In less than an hour, she'd slip inside our shared room, closing the door behind her with a thump. She'd wiggle into fresh underpants, and leave once again, closing the door behind her with a bang. Each of her entries and exits woke me with a jolt. She had five or six meetings that night, leaving the rest of us with little sleep.

I lit a candle in Santa Maria Novella, climbed to the top of the Duomo in Florence, and marveled at mosaics in Ravenna. A friend treated me to dinner in a castle, where we dined on duck (five courses of duck!), including a duck dessert. We ate in the world's first enoteca or wine bar in Ferrara, Italy.

Venice's gondolas and canals lured me in, until the hotel, where my friend had reservations, told us they were full. By my writer friend was resourceful and spoke some Italian, so we ended up in different hotel in a room with a view. In a shoe store, a store assistant lowered the window blinds for privacy before we tried anything on. I left with a pair of beautiful black leather boots that eventually wore out.

Near the end of my trip, on a train ride to Rome, an Italian man in his forties with a strong nose and a face I wanted to draw shared the story about how his marriage dissolved. He looked out the window at the rolling countryside as the train bumped along the tracks, clickety clack, and he sighed. "I don't understand why it happened. I was the best husband I could be. I have no idea what to do with my life now."

I nodded. "I know what you mean. I was married

before and divorced, and starting over is hard to do. But it's possible."

He said he was offered a position at the World Bank in Washington, D.C. but he was hesitant to move. "But nothing is holding me here anymore, now that she left me."

"I think you should move," I said. "Go ahead, take the job."

He told me how Hannibal crossed the Alps with his war elephants, climbing a treacherous pass. He acted out the part of an elephant finding footing on a steep rocky slope, and we got off the train, going our separate ways. But every now and then, I wonder if he accepted the job and opened his heart again.

2

THE DORM

I attended a small college in Wisconsin for freshman year, and I asked the track coach if I could join the team. I went running with my brother Bob in high school, one time after consuming a big ice cream sundae, and I wanted to continue doing that.

The coach cocked his head. "Join the track team? We only have a men's team." He rubbed his chin and said, "But come to think of it, Title Nine just came into effect."

He put his hands on his hips and nodded. "Sure, you can join the team."

I ran with the guys and soon pulled in two female friends to run with us. At a Chicago AAU meet, I won first place in the Women's one-mile race walk, but I was the only contestant. I didn't place in the 880 race, and a sophomore on the team motioned me over to the wooden bleachers, where he said, "You've got to have a killer instinct. Make a strong finish. Work on that."

A good friend who had joined the track team and ran with me, plodding through snow, encouraged a bunch of us to move from the dorm into another building. I went home for spring break and came back a day early, due to a ride share arrangement, walking down a hall in an almost empty dorm. My footsteps echoed on the linoleum floor. Dorm room doors were closed and locked. My runner friends hadn't returned yet.

I went in my room, closed the door and unpacked my things. A loud knock on the door startled me, and I opened the door to two male students in their mid to late twenties who had served in the Vietnam War.

They shifted from side to side, wearing smirks on the faces. The tall redheaded guy with strong biceps peeking out from his t-shirt pointed down the hall. "Come see my new bedspread. I just bought it."

The short, less muscled man said, "Yeah, it's really cool. You've got to see it."

They motioned to the end of the hall, where the taller man lived. I shrugged and followed them down the hall, past closed doors, in an almost deserted dorm.

Stepping in the taller man's room, I halted just inside the door and glanced at the orange batik print bedspread. "That's nice." I turned to go.

"Take a closer look," the taller man said, coming at me,

making me take a step back. The short one stretched out his arms and blocked the door.

The redhead strode toward me, staring into my eyes, and I moved to the door. In self-defense classes at college, I'd heard one rape happened each week on our small college campus. We learned to place our keys between our fingers and fight, but foolish me, I didn't bring my keys.

The tall guy tried to push me down on the bed, but I yelled, and he blinked. I raced to the door, but the short man extended his arms, barring the exit. I screamed and yanked the door open, running to my room and slamming the door shut, locking it and clenching my fists.

I was lucky to get away unscathed and told my friends what had happened. I watched my back and my friends' too for the rest of the term. The college sent letters to freshman telling us we must attend classes during the summer due to a new fiscal program. I tossed it in the trash and refused to stay. A college official told me, "You can have an exemption if you join the men's cross-country team and run in the fall."

I shook my head. I loved running with the team, but my college experience there was tainted. I wanted to get away and start over somewhere other than this industrial town a few hours away from Chicago.

When a student with a messy mop of brown hair and a wide smile gave me daffodils, a poem he'd written and an invitation to move to Evanston, Illinois to live next door to him, I agreed, opening the next chapter of my life.

But reading this piece, I sigh, because I'm ashamed I didn't think to report the two-man batik bedspread incident to school authorities. I didn't know to do that in 1975. But there are no excuses. I'm deeply sorry.

3

MISSING POLYESTER PANTS

I found a job at the Gap Stores for when I graduated from college, meeting with a Gap District Manager from Seattle on the University of Oregon campus in Eugene. For interviews, I wore a bright yellow polyester pantsuit that I'd sewn. I was hired to be a Trainee for the role of Acting Manager at a Gap Store in Northgate Mall in Seattle, so I moved north.

I was paid what was considered to be a lot of money then, in 1978, with a starting salary of ten thousand dollars a year. So up to Seattle we moved, and the movers we hired weren't very good, because they strapped the mattress onto their truck and it fell off onto the freeway a few times on I-5.

Managers of the Northgate Mall Gap Store came and went, so I was promoted, despite my waving my hand at a district meeting and marking a woman's white silk blouse with a blue ballpoint pen.

One day, I stood at the cash register on a raised platform and a big, beefy man strode into the store, tossing a worn sherpa jacket on the counter in front of me. "I want my money back or a new jacket," he said in a low rumbling voice, staring at me.

Because I was standing on a platform, I was eye level with the muscled man. I examined the sheepskin denim jacket, which was worn through at the collar. I set it down and told him a refund or exchange wasn't possible. He glared. "Let me see the manager."

I pulled myself up to my full height of five-foot-two. "I am the manager."

He eyed the cash register, grumbled and grabbed his old, worn jacket, striding out.

Strange things were happening in changing rooms, where women got on the floor and used pliers to zip up tight pants they were trying on. I became disenchanted with retail sales and working all kinds of hours while my friends worked regular jobs.

We took inventory, and I breathed a sigh of relief. At least that was done. But one day, two matching twin-like men in their thirties with dark hair and blue suits stood in the doorway of the tiny office in back, where I was adding up sales on an adding machine.

"We're from headquarters," one said.

I stood and said hello.

The second man stared at me. "Where are the polyester pants?"

My eyebrows shot up. "We sell jeans. We don't have any polyester pants."

The first man leaned in, pointing at me. "They should be in the basement. They weren't on the inventory count."

My mouth fell open. "I didn't even know we had a basement."

They cocked their heads. "The store room?"

Another employee with bleached blond hair and red long lacquered nails, came by. "Do you want to get into the store room downstairs? I have the key."

I followed them and we went outside, down a set of stairs and along a dark hall into a long, dim room, where a yellow bulb flickered overhead. Ballasts in florescent light fixtures buzzed. The two men examined boxes but found no polyester pants.

One said, "That manager who just left used to sell polyester pants."

His twin said, "Maybe he took the missing pants and sold them at swap meets."

They turned to me, eyes blinking as if realizing I was there. One pointed and said, "Don't tell anyone what you just heard."

They hustled out of the store for the airport, dressed alike, frowning and looking like identical twins. The missing polyester pants incident made me realize I craved more meaningful work, so I mailed a letter with my resume to a man who ran a marketing and economic research consulting firm in Tacoma, Washington. We met when I was in college and working in a small town reached by a covered wooden bridge. It was only later I discovered what lay beneath the surface of his polite, respectful demeanor.

4

BRING YOUR BIKINI

The owner of a consulting firm called me into office. He sat down and motioned for me to close the door. The boss leaned in when I was seated and said, "I'd appreciate it if you wore a bikini on your lunch break and sunbathed on the deck out back. You could be right by my window and enjoy the view looking over the water."

I grimaced and shuddered, biting my lip. This was 1978, and women didn't speak up about strange remarks like this. I needed the job. He waited and leered across the desk, leaning on his elbows. I stood and said, "I'd rather not."

He shrugged. "The other girl before you did it. She didn't mind."

I shook my head. This was getting stranger and stranger. "No."

With a slight smile, he said, "Bring your bikini on business trips and wear it by the pool at the Sheraton in Spokane next week."

"No."

I opened the door and went back to my desk, passing my friend along the way. I rolled my eyes, and she nodded. One of the three male bosses at the company had been making moves on her too. We both needed to keep our jobs to put food on the table, so we couldn't walk out the door at every affront. When one of the men in the firm walked in the door touching his private parts, hoisting them with his hand as he lumbered to her desk, I cringed every time.

I thought I'd avoided a bikini trap, but one day I called in sick with the flu. The next day I returned to work on Ruston Way. Water lapped at creosote pilings, and all was peaceful until I entered the building, and the boss motioned me into his office.

"Sit down," he said in a firm voice, and I slumped in a seat, wondering what was wrong. He sat behind his desk, staring at me. "You called in sick yesterday, but I know it wasn't true, because your husband called here to talk to you. You weren't home, and you were covering it up. You were having an affair, and I knew it." He pointed a finger at me.

I stood and shook my head. "That's not true. I was sick, but he left for work at five in the morning and didn't know

I was too ill to go to work. I was home sick all day, when he was working at the hospital."

"Sit down," he said, pushing his thinning hair back, but I stayed standing by the door. A recruiter recently called looking for someone with my qualifications, and right then and there, I decided to call her back as soon as I fled this ogre's office.

He cleared his throat and patted his paunch. "What I called you in here to say is, if you're going to have an affair, and I know you are. Nothing you say will convince me otherwise. Then have it with me. I've helped other young women in your position before. For the girl before you, I even bought logs to go under her house boat on Lake Union."

I stood stunned, my hands hanging down. He wasn't giving up. I didn't need logs for a houseboat or any other bargain. I opened the door. "I'm not interested."

"Just remember, if you change your mind, I'll be right here. I can help you. And your husband will never find out. We'll keep it a secret, just between us."

I shuddered and strode to my desk in an open work area. Typewriters tapped away, and I called a recruiter for a major regional bank and spoke with her about applying for a market research position. I waited to hear back, and the days ticked slowly by, until disaster struck down the street.

5

THE EXPLOSION

One afternoon, perhaps around three in the afternoon, a bunch of us were at work at the consulting firm on Commencement Bay. All was going well, except for the fact that I'd been turned in by a secretary who wanted my job to the higher ups for not having a big enough vocabulary. I was put on probation because I didn't know the word "ilk."

I learned how to lead focus groups on topics like banking and king crab fishing. I studiously flipped through a word a day calendar and opened the dictionary to random pages, challenging myself to learn new words. "You're off probation," the leering boss told me, so there we were working one afternoon.

A loud boom sounded nearby. Windows rattled. The building shuddered and swayed slightly over creosote pilings in the bay. A murky cloud of brown haze slowly spread over the water.

One of the bosses rushed in, saying the Asarco Copper Smelter maybe a half mile down the street had exploded. I stepped outside and blinked at a brown cloud billowing from a huge smokestack. The sky grew dark. A metallic odor lingered in the air.

I went inside and knocked on the boss's door. He was leaning over his desk, eyes trained on a document. He looked up and frowned.

I said, "The Asarco smelter blew up. I'd like to leave early and go home."

He stood and marched into the main room, saying in a loud voice, "No one is leaving here early today. I don't care what happened. We have work to do."

I sat down and drummed my fingers on the desk, determined more than ever to find a new job. That day, I left promptly at five o'clock and jumped in my car, fleeing for my home in south Seattle.

What metals did we breathe that afternoon? A Washington State Department of Ecology report says arsenic, lead and other heavy metals were dispersed that day, contaminating the air, surface soil, and more than one-thousand square miles of the Puget Sound basin. If you're interested in learning more about it, search for "Tacoma Smelter."

SMALL REGIONAL AIRPORT

My parents cut me off financially when I was in college, but a few years later, my folks told me money in my name was left in my college fund that had been set up my paternal grandparents, my career Army grandfather and jolly grandmother. I decided to use the money to buy a house, although I couldn't pay much.

My boyfriend and I toured a house with a huge crack in the foundation. Another contender was located by a bar on a busy arterial where a shooting recently occurred. In a house on Beacon Hill, an older, wrinkled man sat smoking in a recliner, watching us. A yellow coating of nicotine covered the walls, and I didn't think I'd ever get the smell out.

Finally, the realtor took us to a big yellow house with two bedrooms downstairs and two tiny rooms up a steep set of stairs. Grass in the front yard grew to over a foot tall. Blackberries invaded the back yard. I tromped up the front steps and pointed down the street. "What's that red and white checkerboard down the street? Why is it there?"

The realtor smiled. "That's just a small regional airport."

The house had potential, and I decided to buy it. But I was surprised to learn, in 1978, that a single woman couldn't get a mortgage. I was working and had a pretty good income, but banks turned me down. When I told the realtor about my predicament, she nodded. "I've heard that happens. Sadly, I've seen single men your age making the same amount of money get mortgages from the same banks that turned you down."

She spoke to the owner, who was eager to sell, and he offered me a contract to buy it. We settled in and cut the grass with a contraption we rented that wielded a sharp blade. The kid next door, about age twelve, wandered over and said he was a cat burglar when he wasn't in school, helping break into high rises in Madison Park by climbing up the outside of buildings and slithering through open windows.

Soon, I realized why this yellow house had taken so long to sell. On Sunday mornings, window panes rattled as engines revved and roared a block away at Boeing Field, where they tested planes before sending them all over the world.

At night, planes roared overhead, swooping down,

rattling windows and waking us up. A study of school age children showed their grades suffered from waking up many times in the night by jet noise.

I sold the house three years later, and the buyer paid two times what I had. He wanted to move back to the neighborhood where he'd grown up. I wonder if he still lives there and if he installed triple-pane windows to block out the noise.

I moved into an old Victorian in Seattle, where I walked down a hill to work wearing sneakers, changing into heels at my desk. In the early 1980's, my boss took me aside and told me not to wear sneakers to work, even though I changed out of those and slipped on pumps at 7:30 in the morning.

The Seattle house had two fireplaces and an old octopus furnace that conked out three days after we moved in. A window blinds salesperson stared at our down coats and wool hats worn inside and shook her head. The previous owners moved to Amsterdam, to continue his career as a jazz drummer, and the country-style kitchen featured a drinking fountain, perhaps used by slurping, sweating drumming students.

One evening, I heard a commotion at the front door and went to see what it was. Our dog growled and barked in a frenzied fit. I looked through the locked door but didn't open it. A broad-shouldered man with wild blond hair wearing a backpack was standing on the porch turning the door knob, but it didn't budge.

The stranger said, "Let me in. I stay here when I'm in town."

"The previous owners moved. You have to go somewhere else."

He rapped on the window, glaring at me. "I need to stay here. I always do."

"We live here now. Find another place."

He rattled the door knob, but it was locked. "I just flew in. I'm tired. Let me in."

I held up my hands. "We can't help you."

My dog barked for good measure, and the man turned, stomping down the front steps.

7

SEVENTH GRADE

When I was in seventh grade, my best friend invited another girl to hang out with us. The three of us went to the mall after school and attended dances on weekends. The strange thing to me now, looking back, is how subtly the fabric of our friendship changed. We started stealing booze from our parents to put in prescription pill bottles, which we drank in the bushes after our parents dropped us off at dances. I became queasy and threw up.

My dad thought the cleaning woman was taking the liquor, and he put a lock on the cabinet above the fridge. I waited to tell him I did it until forty years later, and he blinked back tears, saying he was disappointed with me.

When my two friends started taking mescaline and having sex with boys at a Michigan lake cabin, everything shifted, and I stepped back. We were thirteen and fourteen. I don't think their parents had any idea what was going on. When they invited me to come to the cabin over a weekend, I declined.

Seeking out other friends, I struck up a friendship with two other girls, who lived on the other side of town. To see them, I walked five miles, or so it seemed, especially in the snow. The bus rarely came, because in Detroit people were encouraged to drive and buy a new car every two years to support the auto industry. My parents bought a Toyota, and my mom came out of a grocery store to find a note tucked under her windshield wiper blade that said, "Buy American cars. Support your neighbors."

Motown was the other big industry, and as a kid on the playground after school or on weekends, someone would bring a transiter radio and we'd sing along to songs like, "Going to the Chapel of Love."

In high school, I dated a fellow freshman who told me he was a drug dealer. The irony was his father worked with mine at a pharmaceutical company downtown by the Detroit River. I went to a party at a classmate's Tudor-style mansion near Lake St. Clair. When we left, the place was trashed. The parents came home and sent our friend to military boarding school, and we never saw him again.

Deep inside, I had a growing sense that pretty, shiny things wouldn't necessarily bring happiness, and I started attending prayer groups. A good friend told me the National Honors Society at our high school voted not to let me in because I was religious. The fact that I was excluded from an academic group based on my beliefs still frosts me. I was being formed to fight for underdogs, which I do now by writing fiction with feisty characters who right wrongs.

8

A DRAWING IS COPIED

Our assignment in grade school was to make a painting. I bent over the desk, putting a wash of pink watercolor over white paper and adding in bold, black brushstrokes, a profile of a figure of a man with a bulbous nose. I nodded, pleased with my painting.

Our teacher came up the aisle and stopped, staring at my painting and then at my best friend's artwork. She said, "Try not to copy each other. Do your own original work."

I leaned over and saw my friend's painting looked like mine. Deep within, something snapped, and I wanted to protect my ideas and my art, which would forever drive me forward. Of course, the irony is I now realize my painting was derivative of a cartoon, Mr. Magoo, so without knowing it, I was copying too.

In high school photography class, a teacher tugged on his salt and pepper goatee and told me not to plagiarize. I said, "I took a photo of a painting. Why is that wrong?"

He frowned. "It's someone else's work, not yours. Don't take credit for another person's art. The concept of plagiarism is very important. Avoid it at all costs."

At a street fair in Seattle's University District, where my pottery was displayed in my booth, I thought I was being original, but the husband of another artist called me a copycat for decorating my pottery bowls and plates with cats, which his wife did. I thought my calligraphic cats were different enough to be differentiated, but he didn't think so. He sounded like I should avoid all depictions of cats, but now that I think about it, maybe he was right. There was something slightly similar in the facial features of my cats and hers. But wait, that is what cats look like!

Anyway, back to the fair. The lanes between booths were clogged with women walking slowly with friends, chatting about what was new and important in their lives and clutching cups of takeout coffee like they were life rafts. Babies in backpacks dozed, but dogs on leashes whined in the heat, ready to go home. Frazzled couples pushing strollers with small howling children blocked the aisles.

A woman in her early thirties came in my booth, and I stepped forward with a smile, thinking here at last, out of the masses streaming by, was a possible paying customer.

I was hot and tired from setting up my booth at seven in the morning, and it was approaching noon.

Her gaze stopped on a soap dish decorated with my calligraphic-style smiling cat and a matching bowl. She said to a man the same age wearing a polo shirt and shorts, "That's what I'm going to make. I'm going to copy it!"

Before I could stop her, she aimed her camera at the items and snapped a series of photos of my pottery, click, click, click. She hurried away before I could say, "Please don't do that. It's not right to copy someone's art."

But myopia affects most of us. When I was a beginning potter, I imitated my teacher's swooshes of color on black glaze. I approached a gallery in Issaquah and one in Olympia, walking into stores with a bowl in my hand and a car full of boxes of pottery. They both bought from me on the spot, but my teacher must have frowned at how his student was marching around Western Washington selling beginner pots resembling his

When I had a pottery studio in Seattle, business picked up, and I gave birth to twins. A part-time employee wouldn't meet my eyes and finally admitted she bought a pottery kiln and was making and selling soap dishes decorated with cats sitting in tulips, just like mine.

The cookie tin contained less cash when she worked over the weekends. I began to spend more time on Saturdays at my shop, and sales doubled when I was on site. I taught an art class one evening a week in my studio, and my students and I agreed, there are no new ideas under the sun.

9

MOVING DAY

"I'm a minimalist," I told the mover. "I don't have much to move. It'll only take a few hours."

"If that's the case, we'll move you on our day off, on Sunday."

He'd been recommended by someone I worked with, so on Sunday he showed up with a man in his twenties. The younger guy picked up my daughter's pink Barbie plastic play house and sang a little song about being a Barbie girl as he went out to the truck carrying an armload.

Hours later, the mover was not pleased. I vastly underestimated the amount of my belongings. We still had the pottery studio in the garage to move, with bags of clay, wooden ware boards and kiln shelves and the kiln. The truth was, I had a lot of stuff.

Months later, the mover showed up at my house for a pottery show, standing in line to buy a ceramic fish and a pottery bowl. I said, "You spent hours moving me when I said I didn't have much. Take the fish and the bowl for free. Thank you."

10

YOU CAN'T BE A WRITER

When a good friend learned my essays were published and I'd been paid by magazines, her brown eyes narrowed. Sheila, as we'll call her, said, "You can't be a writer."

I cocked my head. "Why not?"

She crossed her arms and leaned against the wall. "Because you don't have a degree in creative writing. You haven't studied it for years."

A headache bloomed, and right then, our friendship withered.

I said, "Magazines published my writing, and I'm getting paid for it. It must be resonating with some people."

She frowned. "Well, you shouldn't be doing it."

She wanted to silence my voice, but I stood steadfast and continued writing. Over 57,800 copies of my first psychological thriller, Shore Lodge, have been down-loaded/sold, and more than 87,900 copies of my books (ten novels, short humorous fiction and brief business books) have been downloaded/sold. Given those numbers, I think we can say my former best friend was off the mark when she told me not to write.

Who would think they have the right to tell another person to stop creating and learning the craft of writing? She wanted to become a published author, and I'm guessing she felt sour grapes and wanted to squelch any competition. Or was she a mean girl disguised as a dear friend?

When I worked as a potter, a fellow artist told me I should go back to school before I could make a living as an artist. I'd studied art in high school and college, among other subjects, and growing up, my mother kept a potter's wheel in the basement, where I'd throw pots and splatter red clay on the floor, giggling with girlfriends, making a muddy mess. His comment only strengthened my resolve to prove him wrong. I'm amazed that supposedly supportive friends feel free to dump cold water on dreams, drowning them with negativity.

11

NEVER WRITE THIS

I pestered my grandmother, who was in a writing group and hinted at a dark family story.

"Tell me what happened," I said.

"I can't. It wouldn't be right."

"But how did he die?"

She leaned in and said in a hushed voice, "No one must ever know this. We kept it out of the papers. Promise me you'll never write about this."

She told me a true story, and I kept my promise. The details aren't in my books, because I don't want fate or my dead grandmother hunting me down and haunting me. But you'll find threads weaving a tapestry in my books, set in a small fictional town, about a close group of friends, love and betrayal, and nerve-wracking, gut-wrenching guilt.

12

THE FORTUNE TELLER

When my life felt darkest, after my second divorce, I was a single mother of two beautiful young children, and I set up my booth at the Fremont Fair one Saturday in June. I was filled with hope that I might be on the verge of starting a new life, and I wanted to sell a lot of my pottery bowls and vases.

Years before, I'd started out selling at this fair after fleeing banking, where everyone was serious and lacked a sense of humor. Glenda and I set our pots and tiles outside a dentist's office, where fairgoers streamed by from their cars.

A woman with a broad, open face and a braid in back said, "Susan? Is that you?"

She was the mother of a former boyfriend back in Michigan, and we went sailing on their boat after prom.

She'd been my first official pottery teacher, after my mother showed me how to shape a bowl on a potter's wheel. In this gracious woman's class, I made a thick-walled, heavy ceramic duck, and I'm surprised it didn't explode in the kiln.

She bought a black-glazed bowl, and I greeted her other son. Seattle felt small back then, where you'd bump into people you knew all over the city by chance, although because of Microsoft, swarms of new shiny BMWs flew across on the freeway.

In my first foray into selling at a street fair, I sold many pots that day. It was better than begging on a street corner with a porcelain hand thrown plate in my hand, asking passersby on a Sunday afternoon by the bank parking lot to buy a plate so I could eat.

Being older and perhaps not much wiser in the ways of love and relationships, I set up my booth and put out my wares, greeting other vendors and artists in the fresh morning air. The forecast called for sun, and I wore a sweatshirt over a pink flared skirt and a tank top. Every artist feels before we dive in to paint on canvas, work in clay or write a book, that this is the day where everything will be different. This will be the start of something new and better, the day my luck turns.

Heavy dew covered the ground. Cold pavement beneath my feet promised a cooler day than weather fore-casters predicted. I moved my car and parked it blocks away, hoping I'd remember where it was later.

Metal pipes clanged on the ground as artists set up booths. Plastic tarps flapped in a breeze coming off Puget Sound and rushing west. Greeting cards in the booth opposite me fluttered and flew away toward the canal, and the artist rushed over to retrieve them.

People streamed by, couples smiling, walking hand in hand, women pushing whining children in strollers, or joggers dragging dogs on leash through the crowd. Another artist offered to spell me at my booth, and I trotted off to a foul-smelling porta-potty. Holding my breath and coming outside, a fortune teller's table caught my eye.

I patted my money belt and studied a sign on the green card table. Ten dollars for a reading. My gaze flicked back at my empty booth. This was a good time, if I was ever going to do this. The chair in front of the fortune teller was empty.

My pulse picked up, and I strode over to the fortune teller. She looked up with a smile, blinking heavily outlined dark eyes. Metal bracelets jangled on her wrist as she beckoned me closer. I hesitated. This seemed like a foolish way to spend money.

"Sit, sit," she said, pointing to a folding chair in front of her. "Are you a vendor here? An artist?"

I beamed. "Yes."

"I'll give you a discount. Five dollars for you."

I sat, touching the cards as instructed, and heard her

say, spreading out the deck, "I see a bridge of hearts made whole. I see great happiness in your future."

I stood up and thanked her, heading back to my booth and holding that vision for many years. And it all came true, every last bit of her prediction.

Next up is Book 3, *Canoe*, in the *Strangers on a Train Series.*

CANOE

TRUE STRANGE TALES

1

SWIMMING

When I was about five years old, I waded into Lake St. Clair in Michigan on a summer day. My mother sat on the beach reading. My two older twin brothers weren't there.

I don't recall a life guard being on duty at the little beach next to a park. I wandered out into the lake, feeling my way along on the muddy bottom. The water level rose, up to my knees, my thighs and hips. All of a sudden, the ground dropped off beneath my feet.

My heart raced, and I tried to doggie-paddle back to where I could stand, but I sank down into the murky water, clawing and gasping for air.

A red two-piece swim suit swam by, and I grabbed onto the swim suit bottom with an iron grip, grasping it with all my might. She struggled and tried to push me off, but I held on. She dragged me to shallow water, plunking me down.

My chest heaved, and I blinked back tears.

She spluttered. "You dragged me down. Why'd you do that? I almost drowned."

Tears streamed down my cheeks. "It was too deep."

"Don't go in there if you can't swim."

She stormed off into the water, and I stood slack-jawed and trembling. I glanced back at the beach, where my mother was bent over a book, turning the pages. I never told her what happened.

2

CANOE

My earliest memory is of a girl being carried away down a long, dark tunnel. I reached out to save her, but I couldn't stop what was happening. She was gone, and I was alone..

As a child, I had what I called 'gray dreams' that I told no one about, reliving that moment and waking up weeping in the mornings, struck by a chord of losing a dear friend. Images of a girl disappearing, despite my trying to rescue her, haunted my dreams.

One day when I was a teenager, my mother mentioned how she had carried a heavy wooden canoe when she was three or four months pregnant with me. She bled and bled and lost the baby. A doctor told her she had miscarried. But a few weeks later, she discovered she was still pregnant with a child, who turned out to be me.

Some experts believe children retain memories from being in the womb, like seeing my twin pulled away in utero. When my own twins were little, I overheard my daughter say to my son, 'You kicked me when we were in Mama's belly. Stop it."

3

MY FATHER'S SECRET TWIN

My father took me aside one day and told me a story about his being a twin. I don't recall if this was when I was growing up with twin brothers and asking pesky questions, or if it was after I gave birth to twins. If you ask my mother about this, she'll say she doesn't remember this, but here is the story Dad told me at least two times.

He was sitting in our back yard in a suburb of Detroit with his parents, who were visiting from Colorado. My older brothers were just born, and Dad said to his folks how it was amazing he and my mom had twin boys, because twins don't run in the family.

My grandmother grew silent and dabbed at tears in her eyes.

My grandfather, a tough Army career man who had

been missing in action for two years in the South Pacific during World War Two, blinked back tears.

Dad asked what was going on, and my grandmother said, "Eddie, you were a twin, but we didn't tell you. Your twin was stillborn and desiccated at birth."

Dad emphasized the word *desiccated* each time he told the story, and I had to look it up in the dictionary the first time I heard it. It means dried up. He blinked back tears and told me how he grew up missing a boy he had played with when he was young, but the child left. My father was a man of facts, and he felt the loss of his dead twin brother.

I'm glad Dad told me his tale, but I never said I also had an emotional memory of my missing twin. It was his story, and he rarely shared naked emotions, so I wanted to be a blank canvas for him and just listen. I said, "I believe you. Thank you for telling me,"

After my father's memorial service, a family member asked my mother if Dad had a twin. Mom said she hadn't heard this story from my dad and maybe she wasn't present during the discussion in the back yard when my brothers were babies.

I'd like to go back in time and take him aside, telling him I understood because it happened to me. But it's too late to do that now, and all we have left are his ashes.

4

POTTERY KILN

When I was married to a man we'll call Starlight, because we met on a night when the stars were out and meteor showers filled the sky, I moved my pottery studio home when my gift shop studio floundered. Sales slacked off at my shop because the concept of simplified living without giving gifts spread on Phinney Ridge in Seattle, where many of my customers lived, and the city replaced the sewer line in front of my shop, closing the street for months. My customers shopped elsewhere.

Our marriage bumped along, despite him saying he had a secret with the babysitter. I asked what it was, but he wouldn't tell me. I was taking care of our kids, making pottery and writing. If we went out with other couples, he told me to only mention I was a mother. I tried it at a dinner downtown before a show, when a well-dressed woman asked what I did, and hearing my reply, she turned to the person next to her and ignored me the rest of the evening.

One day, I checked our bank balance with the hopes that we'd saved enough to dump the problematic car I was driving, which broke down on I-90 when I was with our kids. Another time, a man pointed to my car and yelled, "Your car is leaking gas." I took it to a mechanic, who confirmed the gas tank was leaking. When I told my then husband, he shrugged said he suspected as much.

I checked our savings account balance to see how close we were to buying a different, used car for me. A bank teller told me the account had thirty dollars.

I said, "But we had over ten thousand dollars in the account. Please, check again."

She pursed her lips and nodded, looking at a computer screen. "Yes, the savings account has thirty dollars in it."

"What happened? Was there a withdrawal? I didn't take money out."

She cleared her throat. "The other account holder withdrew ten thousand dollars, but at least he left you some."

My mouth fell open. "Can you get the money back? I didn't authorize it."

She shook her head. "It's a joint account, and the other account holder has the right to withdraw money."

I gritted my teeth and left. When I slept, I dreamed of being in prison. I packed a go bag for myself and my kids and stored it at a friend's house. When I confronted him about the withdrawal from our joint savings account, a slight smile flickered across his face before he wiped it away. He said, "I thought you were acting crazy, so I did it."

I filed for divorce. One evening, I went into the garage to check on a kiln I was firing. I put my hands on my hips and stared. The kiln was unplugged from the wall. Only one other person, the man I was married to, had access to this locked space.

I bent down, plugging in the kiln, and started the firing from the beginning, slowly warming clay pots and bringing them up to bisque temperature.

From then on, I watched his movements to make sure he wouldn't sneak into the garage and sabotage a kiln firing. When I confronted him, he shrugged and walked away in an ultimate power play, wielding silence as a weapon.

My lawyer drew up divorce papers. A publisher asked for a manuscript with my essays for possible publication. Sleeping in a separate bedroom, I'd look out the leaded-glass windows and send a wish and a prayer that all would be right and bright for my children's future and, somehow, we'd manage to start a new life.

Weeks later, I served him divorce papers and went out to the garage, where I was firing a kiln full of vases and bowls. A fierce red orange glow blazed in the crack between the kiln lid and the thick walls. I'd never seen the kiln this hot before.

My eyes darted around for the source of the trouble and landed on a board leaning against the firing mechanism, blocking it from falling and automatically shutting off the kiln when it reached temperature.

I shoved the board aside, and the metal mechanism dropped down with a thud. I clicked off temperature dials on each of the three levels, but it was far too late. I knew from working at a group studio that the pottery inside the kiln, and maybe even the shelves, had probably melted. Crying wouldn't help, but distance would.

I stomped into the house and screamed at him to move out. The next day, I opened the kiln and found melted pots and slumping ceramic shelves, which I tossed in the trash.

My divorce attorney called soon after to say I was asking for too much. I shouldn't need child care for three hours a day to job search in quiet. I changed lawyers and learned from a mutual friend that my lawyer typically sided with men in divorce cases because of what happened to her husband during his divorce.

It takes two people to make a marriage fall apart, and I know I wasn't a perfect partner. Years later, I wrote a letter to Starlight man, apologizing for my part, but I never heard back.

When I take our dog on walks now, I glance across the

water to a nearby island, where my former in-laws' ashes are scattered, I was told, at the top of a hill.

I nod and continue on my way, breathing in briny air and feeling grateful that I got away to start a new life. I never did find out what his secret was, by the way, with the babysitter, but maybe it's better not to know.

5

HALIBUT

When my twins left for college years later, I moved into my trumpet-playing boyfriend's house. I came home from working at a biotechnology company in Seattle, greeted a parent waiting in the living room, and tossed my purse on a chair in the kitchen. In the music studio across the hall, a fifth-grade student honked and wheezed his way through a trumpet lesson. I rolled up my sleeves and started to make dinner, so it would be ready when Jerry finished teaching for the day.

In the tiny kitchen, I pulled a packet of halibut from the freezer and followed cooking instructions on the package. I used whatever was in the refrigerator, and soon the kitchen was filled with pungent battling fumes of baking fish, boiling cauliflower and instant mashed potatoes from a box in the pantry cupboard.

The studio door opened, a student clomped down the hall to the living room, and I heard the mother speaking with Jerry before the front door closed. The house grew quiet. Dinner odors hung heavy in the air.

I turned off the burners under the mashed potatoes and cauliflower, opened the oven door and checked the fish, nodding to myself. It was a strange, smelly dinner, but he was going to be happy I had cooked. This was the beginning of a wonderful life together.

He came in the kitchen, wrinkled his nose, waved a hand in front of his face and flipped on the fan above the stove. "What's that smell?"

I smiled. "I made dinner."

I served up fish, cauliflower and mashed potatoes, setting down plates at a two-person kitchen table. A dog next door barked from his position on the outside back steps.

Jerry thanked me for making dinner and took a bite of fish, slowly chewing. I did the same and found the halibut tasteless with an unfortunate rubbery texture.

He swallowed several times and coughed, looking like he might throw up. He spit something into his napkin. "Maybe it needs to cook more."

I set my fork down. "It tastes freezer-burned. How long have you had it?"

He stood, putting his portion of fish back on a baking sheet. "I have no idea. It could've been years, because I hate fish. Do you want yours cooked more?"

He baked the rubbery halibut longer, but it didn't improve the flavor or texture. Glancing at each other over plates filled with pungent overcooked cauliflower, bland mashed potatoes and slabs of freezer-burned fish, we stood and dumped our dinners into the trash can under the sink. The dog next door barked with disapproval.

But the story has a happy ending, because we were married and moved to a small town, where Jerry cooks delicious dinners, leaving me with time to write.

"That all-white meal," I say every six months or so. "Wasn't it awful?"

"It was," he replies. "I never want to eat that again."

6

DRAWING ON THE FLOOR

My fraternal twins were boisterous, and I had to watch them carefully, or trouble would break out. But one afternoon, the phone rang, and I chatted for ten minutes with a writer who didn't think I should be published until I earned a Master's degree in creative writing. My children were laughing and loud in the next room. I watched them and listened to my friend talk.

She said, "Can't you make them be quiet?"

"I've tried, but it doesn't work. They're just loud. Got to go."

"Can't you talk for twenty minutes?"

I shook my head. "I can't, sorry."

I hung up and glanced in the sunroom, where my two were sitting on the floor. When I went closer, I gasped.

They'd drawn in oil pastels on the new engineered hardwood floor, using swoopy, artistic lines. I frowned and shook a finger at them. "We don't draw on the floor." Little did I know they had more mischief in store for me.

7

SKATING ON BUTTER

Another time, when my red-cheeked, chubby-fingered twins were three years old, nature's urge hit, and I rushed to the bathroom, saying, "I'll be right out."

I heard squeals of delight through the closed bathroom door and rolled my eyes. What were those two up to? It took me back to my childhood, growing up with twin brothers uniting against me, in a two against one dynamic. I washed my hands, strode into the kitchen, and skidded, almost falling back on my butt, on the slippery surface.

My mouth fell open, and I gripped the edge of the counter. "What did you do?"

My daughter smiled. "We skated on the floor."

My son grinned and held up a mostly used stick of butter. "Using butter."

I looked at the ceiling and thought, give me strength. I was running on fumes, because my daughter woke up screaming every few hours at night, and I'd go running down the hall to see what was wrong.

"We did this room too," my kids said, pointing to the dining room wood floor. "And over there."

The sunroom floor was once again smeared with a substance, but this time, instead of oil pastels, they'd used butter.

I groaned and rested my head in my hands. They were speedy, whipping around, and moving fast. I was raising wild animals, and I needed to be a better circus trainer.

Photos taken in those days show my son a foot off the ground. They were jumping and hopping, fleet of foot and joyous. When I taught them to meditate, they calmed down, and I wrote about it in what became one of my first published essays.

8

MEDITATING WITH TUMBLING TODDLERS*

Whenmy twins were babies, I considered mediating but chose to sleep instead. Over time, however, I became restless. I realized that I had forgotten how to focus and quiet my thoughts. So when my children had their second birthdays, I thought, "Enough. Time to start again." And I returned to meditation.

At first, I thought that meant being alone in silence. But now, after two years of mediating and being a parent, I have become more flexible. I am willing to include my children as I sit, and I have also grown accustomed to their interruptions.

Early on, when my son and daughter played after breakfast, I tried to sneak off alone. But they sensed my absence and sought me out. They knocked on the closed bedroom door and then walked in. I explained what I was doing and ushered them out. They bickered noisily in the hall, their voices amplified by the walls and wood floor.

After a few attempts, I began to meditate while they slept. But I missed the time of sitting quietly after breakfast. When I skipped meditation in the morning, I noticed that I often became lightheaded from the commotion of getting the kids off to preschool.

When I tried to meditate, my children were drawn to me, attracted by the rarity of my sitting still and by their power in interrupting a silent person. Until I began to blend meditating with parenting, I had always busied myself around them with constant tasks: folding laundry, washing dishes, or getting ready to go out.

One day, I decided to experiment. I told my kids, "After breakfast, you can join me in my room to meditate, if you're quiet and polite." Then I went into my bedroom and sat on a small red rug. My children tiptoed into the room, and I welcomed them.

Together, we sat cross-legged, or "crisscross applesauce," as they call it. We whooshed air out of our lungs and sat abreast facing the window facing west. They enjoyed being included in my ritual and sat silently for four or five minutes.

This went on for a few months. But by then, my children's curiosity was sated and the novelty was gone. They began to talk while I focused on a far pine tree. Short silences were sliced by arguments about who would sit on which side of me. Hushing them had little effect. I realized then that if I was strident about absolute quiet, the idea of mediating might become negative.

Instead I decided to appreciate even two minutes' silent meditation. I'm now willing to let the children sit on my lap or bump against my knee as they settle into centering, After more than a year of meditating for a few minutes at a time, my children know how to slow their breath and relax if they are sick or upset.

Once while vacationing in California, we discovered a sliver in my daughter's foot. Seeing swelling and redness, we took her to the hospital, where an emergency room doctor examined her foot. He strode off to gather staff to hold down her foot, so he could remove the splinter.

When the doctor left the room, I told her, "If you use your deep breathing and relax, they probably won't hold you down." Like many of us, she doesn't like to be restrained. She let the air flow from her lung and slowly breathed in.

The doctor returned with tweezer, a scalpel, a magnifying glass, and three assistants. I said, "I'd like you to try this first without holding her down. She knows how to breathe deeply and relax."

The doctor lifted his eyebrows and looked at my three-year-old daughter. "Okay, we'll try it." He dug into her trembling foot and freed the sliver. She remained calm, while the three helpers stood by unneeded.

Many benefits have come from sitting together. My children have learned that they can calm themselves, and

I've learned that within two or three minutes, I can focus and become centered and relaxed. Now that I'm a mother, meditation time has become more valuable for me, even when I share it with tumbling toddlers.

(*Previously published in Mothering Magazine.)

9

JOE IS MARRIED TODAY

My twins were taking a nap one afternoon, and I sat in a sunbeam on the wood floor, crossing my legs, slowly breathing. Looking out the window at a blue sky, I emptied my mind, but a strange stray thought flitted through my mind. 'Joe is married today.'

I blinked and stared at an apple tree, shaking my head. That was odd. Where did that thought come from? I hadn't spoken to my high school boyfriend in eight or ten years.

I wrote it off as bizarre and carried on with my life. But I did note the date. It was April twenty-eighth, or there abouts, when the weird thought snaked through my mind.

Two months later, I was selling my paintings and pottery at the Fremont Fair. A man came up to me and turned to be a former high school friend from Michigan.

He mentioned our mutual friend, Joe, and how he'd recently been married.

I held up an index finger. "Did he get married on or around April 28 by chance?"

Our mutual friend's jaw dropped. He leaned in. "How did you know? You must have heard it somewhere."

I shook my head. "No, we haven't been in touch for years. It just came to me one day. If you see him, tell him hi from me."

He shuddered. "That's just spooky, if you ask me." He turned and walked away, blending into the crowd passing by.

10

PREDICTION

When I told my maternal grandmother that I was getting married to my college boyfriend, she didn't miss a beat before saying, "You'll divorce. Mark my words."

I gripped the telephone tight, believing she had a powerful gift of intuition. Before the Great Depression, she had pleaded with my grandfather to move their money from a U.S. bank to a Canadian bank, which he did, two days before the stock market crashed.

I said in a teary voice, "Why did you say that?"

"You come from different religions. It won't work. When you divorce, come to me, and I'll help you."

I hung up and put my head in my hands, weeping. How could someone who loved me put a curse on our marriage? She refused to attend the wedding, so we went ahead with out her, holding it in a Seattle park looking over the water. It began to rain before the service, little drops drizzling down, and the violinists we'd hired moved their chairs and played from under the branches of a tree.

For some strange reason, we decided to hold the reception many miles away at a now-burned down Mountaineer Lodge on Snoqualmie Pass. It was a pain for everyone to get there, including the polka band. The chocolate fountain was a hit, as was my sister-in-law's fabulous cake. Our honeymoon started in Victoria, Canada, and we bicycled for miles, camping along the way.

But years later, we split up for many reasons, and I dialed my grandmother's number with trembling hands from a studio apartment, where I shared the kitchen with a sturdy family of cockroaches who refused to be evicted.

After we said hello, I told her we'd broken up and were divorcing. I said in a tight voice, looking down on the bank building next door, "You said when we divorced you'd help me out with money. Could you please do that? I need your help."

She said in a crisp, clear voice, "I can't do that. It wouldn't be right. If I did, I'd have to help all my grandchildren."

She hung up, and I glanced around my tiny apartment, which housed my booth and boxes of pottery and a foldout sofa bed. I nodded to myself. I was going to find a way to rebuild my life somehow, some way, without her help. My grandmother and her cousins the cockroaches couldn't hold me back.

11

ELECTRICAL CURRENT

We walked side by side during a dinner break during a two-day conference, passing a group pottery studio by Seattle Center where I'd once worked. I glanced at a spot in a parking lot by the brick building where three men lifted my friend Gary's motorcycle onto a pickup truck, stealing it, despite it being locked up with chains, but I didn't mention it to my walking companion. We'd just met at the meeting, and I didn't want to babble or bring up personal remembrances.

We walked past what was then the Coliseum, and he said, "I'm a masseuse, but it's been difficult. Not many clients like my touch."

I cringed. Was I walking with a weirdo? Maybe I needed to cut the break short and hoof it back to the conference early. But the fresh air felt good, after sitting inside for so long, and he seemed like an okay guy, despite my imagination racing ahead into dark wooded areas, where I'd end up dead and laid out on a morgue slab. Plus, I was curious.

"What do you mean?" I asked, wondering if his hands were course and calloused, or his fingers were sweaty. It was a strange conversation, but I wanted to know what was wrong.

He said, "Dating is difficult, for the same reason."

I frowned. This was definitely weird. I picked up my pace, but said, "Why?"

He kept up with me, striding easily, matching me step for step. "I give off a magnetic field."

I stopped under a streetlight and stared at this regular-looking guy with brown hair and brown eyes, wearing a jacket, jeans and sneakers. He could be anyone. He didn't stand out. He looked absolutely normal in every way. "You do?"

"Yeah."

"Really?"

He nodded, holding up his hands. "People feel a shock when I touch them, like an electrical zap."

My jaw dropped open. I finally said, "That would make it difficult to be a masseuse, I guess."

He swallowed, and his Adam's apple bobbed up and down. "Can I try it on you?"

My eyebrows shot up. "Okay, I guess." I tensed my muscles, bracing myself. "Go ahead."

"Here we go." He slowly raised his left hand and gently touched my shoulder.

With a sudden zap, a jolt of electrical current raced through me. I flinched and frowned at the unfamiliar sensation. It was jarring, mysterious, and most unpleasant.

He shook his head. "I had to try. Sorry about that."

I stepped back. "Wow, that was something. I felt it, but I wouldn't want to do it again. It's amazing you can do that."

"It's a hassle to live with. When I touch electrical appliances, they stop working."

"That's sounds awful, but thanks for telling me about it."

"I don't share it with many people. They react like you did and don't like it."

"It sounds like a burden and a gift."

He issued a choked chuckle. "Except I can't find how to use it."

We walked back to the conference we were attending at Seattle Center and never saw each other again. I think of him and his special gift now and then, because for a few years, my dad bragged about how he gave off an electrical current. He said he turned off blood pressure monitors, EKG machines and other medical equipment just by walking into a room, but when I asked him about that six months before he died, he acted like he'd never told those stories.

I've heard human bodies have electrical fields, but some of us must have higher voltage than the rest. The man walking down the street with me that evening didn't have a build-up of electrons on his skin from friction. He was always like that, he said, and what a burden it must have been.

It's too bad we didn't keep in touch because years later, I met a woman with a similar ability who sends out shocks from her fingers. Watches don't work on her wrist. Computers last a year, if that.

Maybe those two would've gotten on well and had babies who sent out currents of electricity through their chubby little fingers. I hope he found happiness, alone on an island with his electrical field and a special gift that few wanted to share.

12

ANGEL'S WINGS

I sidled up to a four-year-old girl in my summer clay camp. She was bent over the table, frowning and forming something. I glanced at my watch. Parents were due any minute to pick up their kids.

She'd been quiet all day and had missed class the day before. I bent down and said, "You look like you're making something very special."

She nodded but didn't look over, her little fingers carefully smoothing out the red terra cotta clay. She whispered something that I couldn't hear, so I said in a soft voice, "I didn't hear you. What did you say?"

"I'm making angel's wings. My nanny died."

I pursed my lips and was quiet for a beat, not expecting to hear that. "Well, you're doing a good job. Keep it up."

She whispered. "I'm almost finished."

When her mom came in later, I took her aside and told her what her daughter had said. Her eyes grew wide. "She told you that?"

I nodded. "She did. Did someone die?"

"Her nanny died a few days ago. It's hit her harder than I knew."

She put her arm around her little girl and they left, walking out slowly, leaning against each other. I wonder if that death left a mark on the child that would remain for the rest of her life, because of something that I saw one day at summer camp.

I ditched a camp in Georgian Bay, Ontario when I wasn't awarded a Pine Tree pin and someone else received it. (I see you, Suzanna Green!) Instead, I went to summer camp in Wisconsin and landed a part in the musical, Oklahoma, where I sang off-key and was flat. Birds sang. A meadow was beautiful. We played "mumbly peg," throwing pocket knives into the dirt.

One day the bell rang, announcing a group of campers coming back from a canoeing trip. On a typical day, the bell rang, and we'd rush down to the river to wave to the returning group and sing to welcome them home. But the girls in the canoes didn't smile that day. They didn't tap their paddles on the gunnels in unison, like we always did. They didn't wave.

They paddled slowly, not looking at us. Their faces were stone. One girl was missing, and that was when I saw a body in a tarp in a canoe, back by a counselor paddling at the stern.

The camper had been swept under rushing water in a stream, pulled under by the current. She was there one moment, gone the next.

I'll never forget the sight of those canoes coming back, and the somber, solemn grim faces. For years, I wondered how that incident impacted the lives of campers on the fateful canoe trip. Eventually, I wrote a speculative psychological thriller, *Cabin Eight*, that explores the theme of how young tragedy can leave a lasting mark, and how one might be forced to face our fears and shrug it off.

Next up is Book 4, *Soup Kettle*, in the *Strangers on a Train Series*.

SOUP KETTLE

TRUE STRANGE TALES

1

SOUP KETTLE

Things had not been going well. When he threatened to throw himself into a crevasse on Mt. Rainier, I cancelled the climbing trip. I waited until he felt better before I left him.

I moved into a studio apartment but came back to hold a garage sale, where not much sold. In the house, he raised his voice and came toward me carrying an empty soup kettle. In a flash, he tipped it over and put it on my head.

It was dark in the soup pot, and I blinked, stunned at how our love melted down into this moment. He banged on the sides of the kettle with a spoon, and metal reverberated, ringing in my ears. I admit I kept the jointly-owned luggage too long, and I should have returned it before his business trip. He had a right to be angry, because I'd busted up our relationship. I wanted him to get a job and stick with it. I didn't want a three-some when he suggested it. But the soup kettle and banging spoon was over the top.

I took the pot off my head and laughed, and he joined in.

And now we're friends.

2

FOOD ON MY HEAD*

Mashed avocado with lemon juice, cool and green, sits on top of my head. Last Monday night, olive oil and fresh rosemary oozed from my scalp into my eyes, as I massaged a mixture of oatmeal, yogurt and salt in circles on my face.

As my fortieth birthday approaches, I'm assessing my outlook on life and my appearance. Recently, I decided to nurture myself on Monday nights by soaking in a candle lit bath or trying facial scrubs and hair conditioning ideas in magazines.

For three years, I watched my young twins apply lumpy oatmeal, applesauce and spaghetti on their tresses. I've marveled at their soft, shiny hair. To clap this goop on my head is on my wild side. It's almost a dinner, a friend joked. But wild beauty has its drawbacks.

"Leave on for five minutes," the beauty article said, but

didn't mention that mini-oatmeal mountains would slide off my face onto a red oriental rug as I stepped toward the bed to await a five-minute miracle. Despite the mess, my face did look clear and rosy.

One evening, I simmered olive oil and fresh sprigs of rosemary in a saucepan, and the smell permeated the house, whetting my appetite for a feast. I poured warm oil on my hair and wrapped my head in a shower cap, with a towel over that. Oil slid down into my right eye. I washed my hair three times to remove the oil, but it did make my hair shiny.

Tonight, I'm applying mashed avocado and lemon juice on my hair, making me look like a green-headed sea monster. A baby sitter from Chile recommended the recipe when my kids were babies, but I lacked time then to mash avocado on my head.

A hairdresser looked down at my head and said, "Looks like you have dandruff. Do you have any stress in your life?"

"Yes," I whispered.

"Will it end soon?"

"I don't think so."

Tears streamed down my cheeks, and I closed my eyes, fearing I'd bust apart as she scissored my hair.

This goop and glop affirms the healing taking place in my soul, a symbolic way of saying yes to renewal and letting go of the past, although avocado's muted green isn't my best color.

A friend of mine recently died, and in grieving his death, I embrace what I take to be his message for us all. Be wholly yourself, no matter how strange that may be. My friend was like no other. He was not afraid to be completely himself. He made no attempt to mask his oddities.

He ate salad with his fingers to better feel the texture and taste it. His mango eating was full of gusto. He crafted sculptures of sticks from clay. He had protruding ears, but he didn't care. He was himself.

I hope to be more of who I am with fewer apologies. Perhaps putting food on my head is a first step. My friend lived as he liked and followed his heart. With mundane acts of food on my head, I connect with joy, nurture myself, even at home on a Monday night.

(*Written years ago.)

3

BLOOD DRIPPED DOWN

My maternal grandmother paid for my short stories when I was in fourth grade, to encourage me to write. She might have paid a quarter, but the amount doesn't matter. One afternoon, we sat on her floral upholstered sofa in her living room. Light streamed in, and birds chirped outside. I smiled as she read my story, because I liked the plot and thought my writing was improving.

She set down the hand-written story and wrinkled her nose. Pushing the pages aside, she said, "I don't want to read your writing ever again."

My throat tightened with tears. I didn't understand. She'd been encouraging me to write. What had changed?

She tapped a finger on the lined paper. "Blood, I don't want to read about that."

In the story, blood dripped down from the attic into the dining room. The main character Caroline hung from a rope in the attic. She crumpled up my story.

She said, "I don't want to read anything you write again."

4

MISTAKES WERE MADE*

"Prepare for emergency procedures." Those words, uttered by my obstetrician, burst my hopes of having an easy birth for my twins. At the center of the emergency was my daughter, who was experiencing difficulty during her birth and needed help fast.

In just two minutes, my doctor performed a C-section. But my daughter wasn't breathing and had an Apgar score of zero. To save her life, she was placed on a ventilator to pump oxygen into her body.

"Please, be a fighter," I prayed. "Live."

A doctor and nurse came into my room, saying mistakes were made during the birth. Another doctor pleaded with me not to sue Group Health, because their malpractice insurance would go up.

After three days at Children's Hospital in Seattle, she

was still in danger of dying or having brain damage. That night, I had a dream that she would live. She stomped her foot in my dream, wearing a striped blue dress, and said, "I'm strong. I'm healthy. And I'm going to live."

Two weeks after her birth, our daughter finally breathed on her own, and I held her for the first time. A week later, she was released to another hospital, where her twin brother was in a neonatal unit. My daughter refused to drink from a bottle or breastfeed until a nurse broke the rules and took my son out of the NICU, placing him in her bassinet. Their little prematurely born bodies relaxed, with hints of smiles on their faces.

We returned home and weathered two years of quarantine, because the machine that saved her life had forced pure oxygen into her lungs and damaged the remaining lung cells. Doctors told us not to allow visitors in our home from October to June, to avoid colds and respiratory viruses that would threaten her life.

Three years of being in quarantine, living with chronic illness, were a long endurance race. We didn't sue the hospital for malpractice, but there was an investigation, and a physician later told me it was declared the "worst birth" they'd had at the facility.

There aren't do-overs for a bad birth, but I wish there were. Fortunately, my twins lived and are flourishing as adults, despite health challenges. If I could go back and do it again differently, I'd ask my two weeks overdue pregnant OBGYN not to oversee the birth directly, and I'd pipe up early in the thirty-four-hour labor, after my water broke, and say, "Do a C-section now. Get the babies out and don't take chances."

But hindsight doesn't help now. The words of the anesthesiologist still ring in my ears. He came into the hospital room and said, "Mistakes were made during the birth."

Years later, I took my kids to a movie in the University District in Seattle. We waited in line to buy popcorn, and I noticed a woman about my age watching us. She came closer, and I recognized my former OBGYN who had delivered my children.

She stared at my redheaded daughter and said in a soft voice, "That's her, isn't it? She lived."

"Yes, they call her the Miracle Baby at Children's Hospital, because she lived."

"I gave birth in the room next to yours. I could hear you crying."

I nodded. "It was strange to hear you calling out in childbirth, right next door, when I was grieving for my daughter. Doctors said she was going to die."

She sighed, still watching my daughter. "I'm sorry."

We parted ways, and I never saw her again.

What if she'd made a different choice in the operating room and not waited ten minutes before making an incision and pulling out my daughter? What if the two pediatricians on duty (standard operating room practice for twins at that time) hadn't both failed to insert a breathing tube down my baby's throat? What if the nurse on duty spoke up when she thought they waited too long to extract the second twin?

I learned that one person can make a difference, good or bad, even if we have the best intentions. Every action we take, however small, (or if we decide not to speak up and not act) can result in long-ranging consequences, rippling down the line for a lifetime and generations to come. And I learned to be grateful for the good in our lives. We're alive.

(*Previously published and edited for this publication.)

5

DANCING IN A PSYCH WARD

When I was nineteen, I landed a job as an occupational therapy activity aide in a secure psychiatric unit in an upscale nursing home. It was the summer after my freshman year of college, and I rented a room in a house on Orrington Avenue in Evanston, Illinois. Most days, I went to work with a bandana tied over my brown hair and wearing an embroidered peasant blouse, a knee-length skirt and sandals.

Weekday mornings, I led Reality Orientation Therapy sessions with our four most alert residents. They sat in plastic chairs facing a chalkboard in the linoleum-tiled dayroom while others dozed in armchairs. Lawrence was thin and frail. John had broad shoulders, strong hands and a shy smile. In a flowered housecoat, Rose clutched a handbag under her arm. Elizabeth had curly white hair and piercing blue eyes.

Standing before them the first time, my hands trembled. Who was I to lead this class? I'd volunteered in nursing homes during high school, but this was different. I was in a psych ward.

My job was to ask each person for their name and to write it on a chalkboard. Lawrence, John and Rose quickly replied but when I asked Elizabeth for her name, she pressed her lips together and shook her head. She stared, holding eye contact for a beat too long as if pleading with me for something. Her mouth was caved in. Her dentures had been stolen three times, and her family refused to replace them again.

Charging ahead with youth's purpose, I said, "Your name is Elizabeth, isn't it?"

When she didn't reply, I carried on with class. It was part of my job, and I needed to pay the rent.

Rose stood and tucked her purse under her arm. "I need to go shopping." She marched away.

I race-walked after her and gently took her arm, guiding her back to the group. The job was a bigger challenge than I'd expected. Next, I asked my small group to name the president. They sat in silence for a moment.

Lawrence said in a wavering voice, "Ford."

"That's right," I said, writing the name on the chalkboard.

The year was the most difficult question. Time sifted like sand between our fingers in the secure ward. Each second was like the last.

"It's 1975," I said, writing it on the board. "That's all for today. Thanks for coming."

After class, Rose hurried away with her hand bag, while John shuffled off with a slight smile on his lips.

Lawrence said, "Thank you."

"I'm glad to know you," I said, looking into his watery gray-blue eyes and meaning every word. How had he ended up in this locked ward? I wondered what it was like for him to live here.

Elizabeth held my gaze and nodded before going to sit in a chair by the window.

The urge to flee is contagious in a closed environment. For my part, I was glad to leave when my shift ended and go out for a beer with friends. The thin-walled room I rented from a squabbling family wasn't an inviting place to relax after work.

Most afternoons, Rose stood by the sliding glass doors ready to run to the elevator and go shopping. "I have to make dinner," she said.

When I stepped into the elevator at the end of the day, Rose waved from the other side of the glass, as if I was going off on an adventure. I'd wave back and swallow hard. She was stuck inside, but I was heading out for a fun evening. We were bookends in the aging process, and it didn't seem fair.

In contrast to Rose, John managed to slip out and ride the elevator every few weeks. He ambled to a bar a block away for a beer. When the police brought him back, a nurse or aide would throw up their hands and say, "He got out again?" He'd just smile and shrug.

One afternoon, my boss, another aide and I took residents from the independent living first-floor units and three residents from my floor to a classical music concert in a nearby park. My small pod's pace was slow. Every bird and car passing by was a marvel after being indoors. Lawrence eyed each crack in the sidewalk as if it was ready to take him down, but he motored ahead with a steady pace. Elizabeth squeezed my hand and was silent as we went down tree-lined streets. During the concert, Rose hurried off. I ran after her and she came back with me, humming a happy tune.

Some residents belonged in a secure ward. Francis was restrained to an arm chair in the dayroom. When I breezed by, she pointed to a bandana on my head. "Babushka! My name is Francis. I am from Czechoslovakia!"

I patted my head and smiled at her in a kindred spirit kind of moment. But because I'd seen her lash out with hands like claws stopped only by cloth restraints, I stood two feet back.

At lunch one day, I sat with my boss by a window in the dining room. The table was covered with a white linen table cloth. A pewter bud vase held a single red rose. I took a bite of beef stroganoff, and something hurled past the window, looking like a human body.

It hit the pavement with a thud.

My boss and I ran out an emergency exit. Along with a chef wearing a white hat, we were first on the scene. A crumpled human form was splayed on the pavement. Blood oozed out of the man's skull, forming a growing puddle.

A nurse in a white dress ran out and knelt to take his pulse. "He's dead."

I blinked back tears and looked up.

On the fourth floor, a window in a resident's room was open. A nurse in white looked down.

The man on the pavement was Frank, a retired professional basketball player. He wasn't on my floor but I'd heard him yelling at his son when he was wheeled into the nursing home.

"I want to stay home," Frank said. He gripped the wheelchair with veined hands.

His son pushed the wheelchair. "Dad, you can't live at home."

"You can't make me live here."

But his son did. For the short time Frank was a resident, he lived on a floor in the nursing home where residents could come and go. But it wasn't enough for him. He wanted to be home.

Although the window in Frank's room was double-locked, he had managed to pull himself out of the wheelchair, open the window and throw himself out in a desperate final act. I never learned how he managed to open the secure window, but I imagine his determination was fueled by rage at his son's betrayal.

I hadn't known Frank well, but I still felt sick. We needed more joy in this place. I asked if I could play music in the psychiatric unit and dance with residents, and my boss and the charge nurse gave me permission.

Rummaging in a wooden storage unit in the first-floor activity room, I pulled out a portable turntable and hauled it up to the psych ward. I cleared an oval dance floor by moving plastic chairs aside and put on a Hank Williams' album. It was either Hank or Burl Ives, because we only had two albums.

I clapped my hands in the dayroom and defied the stark white walls. On this day, on this afternoon, for just an hour, I was determined for us to experience joy, even if it was from a vinyl easy chair.

"Come dance with me," I called to white-haired, gray-haired and balding residents who dozed in recliners. A few opened their eyes and looked my way. The television droned.

I marched over to the TV and turned it off. "We're going to try something different. Let's dance."

Florence and Marvin sashayed onto the dance floor and moved like practiced ballroom dancers. Elizabeth stood watching at the edge of the dance floor. Rose shuffled over to me with open arms, and we swayed to the music.

At the end of the song, I thanked Rose for the dance and went to find another partner. Extending a hand to Elizabeth, I said, "May I have this dance?"

Her chin trembled, and she nodded as she stepped into my arms. Elizabeth was light on her feet, and she clasped my shoulders like I was a life raft.

While we danced, she rasped in my ear, "My name is Elsie."

Goosebumps pricked my flesh, and a chill ran up my spine. That's why she wouldn't speak. I had the wrong name. It wasn't dentures she'd wanted but to feel loved.

Looking into her sparkling blue eyes, I said, "I'm glad to know your name."

From that moment on, we spoke as if we were old friends.

When Lawrence passed away, his family didn't come to claim his things. Staff members were allowed to select items from his belongings. I took Lawrence's soft blue and white checked shirt as a way to remember him and his valiant courage. Until the end, he was a gentleman of grace in the midst of occasional chaos in the psych ward.

September came, bringing the smell of fall. Oak leaves rustled, awakening in me an urgent need to go to college. On a whim, I picked up the phone and placed calls. Wayne State in Detroit said they'd take me and classes started soon. University of North Carolina in Chapel Hill and University of Colorado in Boulder told me it was possible to get in at the last moment.

When I spoke with the Registrar at University of Oregon, a friendly woman said, "If your grades are as good as you say they are, we'll accept you. Have your previous college send the transcript right away. Classes start in a week."

When I told Elsie, John and Rose about my decision to move to the West Coast, they nodded and looked understanding. But their eyes conveyed a sense of longing, as if they'd like to go with me and have an adventure. And I wish I could have taken them.

The afternoon before I left, I stopped in to see Elsie, who had fallen ill. She was in bed with the sheets pulled up to her chin and her eyes were closed. Taking her hand, I said, "I'll always love you. Goodbye."

Her eyelids fluttered, and she squeezed my hand.

I left her room with a lump in my throat. It wasn't fair that I was able to explore the world while she was locked in a secure ward. I flew away for the both of us and sent her imaginary fragments of the freedom she missed. I later learned she passed away in her sleep several days after I last saw her. I still get teary thinking about her.

Off I went, flying across the country and starting a new life. But those residents in the psych ward are still with me, dancing in my mind. I wore Lawrence's soft blue and white checked shirt for years before finally letting it go, frayed cuffs and all, into the trash. But in a way, I still wear

Lawrence's shirt on my back because knowing him and the other residents changed my life. And I hope I made a difference in their lives too.

(My experiences working in a psychiatric ward influenced my psychological thrillers, *Shore Lodge* and *The Winter Storm*, and you can read more about those brave souls in my books.)

6

MARRIED TO THE SAME MAN

A friend told me her cousin had been married to my ex-husband and showed me a photo of her. At my friend's party, I noticed a woman who might be the cousin, and I took a risk, sidling up to her when she was alone. I said, "I think we were married to the same man."

Her face went pale. Her hands trembled, and she walked toward a table holding bottles of wine. She filled a tall tumbler with red wine and came back to me. "Did he do that thing to you too?"

The room went quiet. No one spoke, and people stared at us, watching and waiting for what we'd say next. A CD of Robert Cray singing crooned in the background, but we'd become the entertainment.

I said in a low voice, "What do you mean?"

She whispered, "You know that thing."

I swallowed, feeling out of my depth, with my imagination running wild.

She sipped red wine and leaned in. "Where he didn't talk to you for days?"

I let out a breath and nodded. "Yeah, he did. It was really strange."

Conversations resumed, swirling around us, and we stepped into a shared weird world, talking for twenty minutes. Later that night, I drove home, smiling and feeling oddly satisfied to have met the owner of the brown leather purse I'd found in his basement, left behind as if she'd fled the premises in a hurry, many years ago.

7

CRACKED GLAZE

A potter I knew in a group studio had smashing success making dinner place settings for couples about to be married. But one day, a couple marched into the studio carrying a plate with cracked glaze. They were unhappy, from what I overheard, and wanted their money back. Most potters were paupers, so that wasn't an easy ask.

A second couple darkened the door of the pottery studio, showing a problematic plate and making the same request, and a ripple of concern ran around the room.

Eventually, the potter left the city and moved to Mexico, never to be found. I was startled by her starting over story and thought it took courage, but it also smelled of running away from problems and leaving others holding pottery with cracked glaze. Little did I know the same problem loomed ahead in my future.

I opened my own studio and small gallery in the Ballard neighborhood of Seattle, and to my surprise and delight, customers lined up to buy pots when I'd open a kiln and unload a glaze firing on Saturdays. It was a potter's dream to sell right out of a kiln.

One day, I opened a kiln and stared at clay pots that had cracked during a bisque firing. Platters pulled apart. Bowls looked like they were ripped on the rims. I had to throw them out. The next batch had the same issue. After some research, I determined that the batch of clay I'd bought must be defective, and it took months for me to convince the vendor that it wasn't my fault. I was sure they left out part of an ingredient when mixing my clay.

When the bad batch of clay was replaced by the company in South Seattle, I thought I'd left my business problems behind. I had attracted a wholesale customer with a friend's help and sold platters shaped like salmon and fish-shaped clocks to a store with many locations.

But the store brought them back. My friend who had recommended me, frowned and said, "They're blaming me for the problem. Customers are bringing them back in droves. The clocks aren't keeping time."

She walked out, and I never saw her again. I called the clock mechanism company, and after three phone calls, they admitted they had substituted a new part in the batch of clocks I bought. They sent a new shipment out, but it was too late. The company selling my fish clocks and platters never wanted to do business with me again. They didn't trust me.

Next, a clear glaze I applied on my pottery started to crack. The supplier blamed me and how I fired the pots, but it had never happened before. Finally, I threw out the jugs of glaze and bought new ones from a different batch.

That was the end of my problems as a potter, I thought, until a man in a blue shirt and khaki pants came into my studio. I smiled and we chatted about the pottery.

He glanced at a bowl, said he liked it, and I said,. "Would you like to buy it?"

He shook his head. "No, I'm here on business, and I'm from the city. I don't know if you heard this, but we're closing the street for sewer repairs, and it'll take a few months."

My throat tightened with tears. I didn't need this. "A few months?"

He nodded. "Maybe more like three or four. We'll see how the project goes."

I swallowed hard, not knowing if my shop could survive a road closure, especially one that long. The construction project took more than four months. When the street reopened, very few customers came in.

Looking at my bank balance and around the empty store, I realized my dream of running a pottery studio and gift shop had run its course. I locked the door and sobbed all the way home.

8

SHOPPING CART

I set up my fair booth at an art show in Gig Harbor, Washington, and a soft breeze blew off the water, pulling tendrils of hair from my ponytail. I placed porcelain pottery bowls on black wire shelves and shoved my hands in the pockets of my green overalls. Glancing at other artists, I smiled. This was going to be a good day for sales. I could feel it in my bones, smell it in the briny sea air wafting past and sense it in the crackling energy around me, as people buzzed about, setting up booths.

A storm had blown through the night before, and wet, cold pavement radiated a chill through my feet. I glanced at a box beneath my table, where foul weather gear was stowed. If needed, I could pull on a rain hat, jacket and pants that I bought from a retired fisherman at a garage sale. I had matching green rain boots at the ready too.

In the first hour or so of the show, I sold a few bowls to

middle-aged women with shoulder-length hair. I was sipping water from a plastic bottle and alone in the booth when something caught my attention out of the corner of my eye.

On the other side of my booth, a metal shopping cart with a young child in the seat was rolling down a slight incline and aiming right for my pottery displayed on wire shelves. The girl, who might have been three or four, watched as she traveled toward my wares. Images of her falling, breaking bones and pottery, flashed through my mind.

I dropped the water bottle and ran around the booth. I lunged forward, reached out my hand and grabbed the back of the shopping cart. It suddenly stopped, just before smacking into my booth.

The little girl sobbed from the jolt. I cooed to her, said it was going to be fine and where was her mother? I craned my neck, searching for a family member. Seconds later, a worried woman in her early thirties trotted over, apologizing profusely and asking her daughter if she was okay.

"Thank you so much," she said. Her eyes fell on my display, and she pointed to a shelf of my work. "I'll buy those." She nodded to another shelf. "And I'll buy those too. I can never repay you enough for saving her."

And that's how she became one of my best customers.

9

WATER EVERYWHERE

My four-year-old twins were quietly reading picture books, and I slipped into the bathroom to take a quick shower. But as I scrubbed, the water pressure dropped. I heard squeals of delight coming from the kitchen.

I turned off the water, wrapped myself in a towel and strode into the kitchen. My mouth fell open. In the matter of minutes, using the sprayer on the kitchen faucet, they had covered the floor, cabinets and windows with water.

"Don't do this again," I said, grabbing a sponge mop and wiping the wet floor. Later, I read in a research study that if you say, "Don't run," some children hear, "Run." Perhaps my mistake was telling them what not to do, instead of making positive statements.

When I mentioned the water incident to a woman, she shook her head. "That's nothing compared to what happened to us. Our twin grandchildren, a girl and a boy, were visiting and playing in the basement. They loaded an entire box of detergent in the washer and turned the machine on. Soap suds filled the basement, and the water was a few feet deep before we noticed. We had to get rid of the washer, which wouldn't work after that. It was a mess to clean up, and it cost a lot!"

She wiped her brow, and we agreed that a special blend of mischief can run in fraternal twins, who often care more about what their twin thinks than adult approval. I knew I needed help to become a better parent, so I signed up for a University of Washington School of Nursing study. They observed us in our "home environment" and suggested I give fewer commands and focus on two or three behaviors I wanted to change, using positive statements and rewards.

I had a binder listing positive behaviors and associated reward points that could be redeemed for TV time, a fast-food meal or cash. Within six months, my kids were on time for the school bus, and they turned in their homework. I just needed a little help to turn two wild hellions into capable future citizens.

10

LAKE CITY WAY

My kids and I left a store on Lake City Way, and my son said, "Watch how fast I can run."

Traffic was stopped at a nearby light, and although he was about four years old, he was fleetingly fast on the temporarily deserted road. I sucked in a breath and took off, calling on all my strength to keep up with him. Pumping my arms, running after him in the road, I tapped my reserves and recalled being on a college track team. I had to grab him before a car hit him. "Come on," I told myself. "Catch him before he's hit."

He ran ahead, feet flying, laughing.

I worried about my daughter, but she stayed on the sidewalk, following us.

Traffic moved, coming toward us, so the light must have changed. The cars could end my son's life, if I didn't save him. Giving it all I had, I leaned forward, grabbed my son and hauled him off the road to the sidewalk, where his sister stood gaping.

Just then, a car chugged by, right where he'd stood moments ago.

Next up is Book 5, *Bathtub*, in the *Strangers on a Train Series*.

BATHTUB

TRUE STRANGE TALES

1

SAFECO FIELD

I walked in the door at half past midnight, tossing my purse and keys on the couch after an evening business event at a ball park. The phone rang as I headed to the stairs to crash into bed. Thinking it must be important for someone to call this late, I picked up the phone. "Hello?"

A man said in a stern voice, "Is this Susan Specht?"

I cringed, hoping no one in my family was hurt. My throat was dry from talking all evening, and I said, "Yes."

"This is Bank of America fraud division. Were you at Safeco Field tonight by chance?"

I rolled my eyes. "Yes, I was there."

"Did you happen to use your credit card?"

I smiled, thinking of the frequent flyer miles I'd racked up. "I did."

"Did you spend ten-thousand-dollars tonight at

Safeco Field? We doubt that's possible and flagged it as fraud."

I grinned. "I did, I spent ten thousand dollars tonight."

"How is that possible?"

"It was a work event, and we rented three suites with catering and a full bar. I paid with my personal credit card to get the frequent flyer miles."

"You spent that much money in one night?"

"Yes."

"All right. If you're sure this isn't fraud, we'll take the flag off your account."

"I'm sure, and thanks for calling. It sounds strange, but it really happened."

"It is most unusual. Goodbye."

We hung up, and I fell into bed, dreaming of trips I'd take with my new frequent flyer miles.

2

A LOVE STORY

A man in a tweed newsboy cap entered my daylight basement where I was holding a pottery show. I was talking with two other customers, but I noticed he opened my bedroom door and glanced in, before my friend told him that was off-limits.

I'd known him for about nine years, and he had been my second-best pottery customer at my previous shop. I kept a running tally, ranked by dollars spent, of customer's purchases, and he came in to buy bowls fairly often to give to musician friends as gifts.

A year before, I had called him to ask if he wanted to go out with my friend, figuring they might have something in common because he played trumpet and she is an artist. After a beat of silence, he said he was giving a trumpet lesson then and that love hurt too much. I winced, said goodbye, and we hung up.

Now, he paused by the table where I stood and picked up a ceramic bowl. He turned to me and looked into my eyes. "Do you want to go out for coffee sometime?"

I didn't drink coffee at the time. I drank green tea. My friend's head whipped around, and she watched us. Conversations in the room stopped.

I leapt into the sudden silence and said with a smile, "Sure, when?"

I'd mailed out postcards announcing the event to customers, and for those who lived within a mile, I added a handwritten note: 'It'd be great to see you!'

I learned Jerry thought this was a personal invitation, a one-of-a-kind come-hither gesture via the postal service. I'd had a crush in junior high on a trumpet player in the band, and it seemed to make sense to go out with him. I'd been divorced by then for two years, and my kids were seven. It smelled of sunshine and roses, as far as I was concerned, until we had our first date.

Instead of coffee, we went out for dinner along the Ship Canal in Seattle. Riding there in his shiny red pickup, he mentioned how he had recently turned fifty, and he wasn't happy about getting older. I bit my lower lip. I'd had a pretty perfect vision of him until this moment, after hearing him talk openly about his father's death. I worried he might be a covert complainer who wasn't content with his life.

We sat across from each other at the restaurant, and I was flustered when I read the lengthy menu, because it had been such a long time since I'd eaten out. I ordered salmon and fidgeted with my hands, feeling more nervous than I had expected.

When he dropped me off and walked me to my door, he asked if he could kiss me. I froze on the spot and said no. He blinked and walked to his truck, and I went inside, locking the door and my heart.

But as the days ticked by, I realized I might have been wrong. First dates bring out nerves. What if my 'man-picker' was broken, and I'd made a mistake? Maybe I'd misjudged him. He was an interesting person who appreciated my artwork. He was a good listener. With my pathetic two-divorce track record, I was hyperalert to potential problems and ready to raise red flags.

Gathering my courage, I picked up the phone and called him to apologize and invite him to Thanksgiving dinner at my house. He said no and quickly ended the call, hanging up before I did.

I went to a performance of the Nutcracker and went up to the railing at intermission with my kids. I glanced at the trumpet section, but he wasn't there. I later learned he hung out in what they called 'curmudgeon corner' with other guys, and he arrived early to make coffee for everyone. I scribbled a note on a piece of paper from my purse and asked another musician to give it to him. Days went by, and eventually, he called.

We went out a few times, when my seven-year-old kids were with their father, who lived a half-mile from me, and

I lived a half-mile from Jerry. At Ray's Boathouse one evening, we sat upstairs in the bar with candlelight, not nervousness, as our companion. He took my palm, drawing slow circles on my skin with his fingertip, giving me goosebumps. Two women at the next table kept glancing over and smiling at us.

But a week later, I asked what he was doing for New Year's Eve, he said he was going to a party on Mercer Island. He mentioned a hand surgeon was hosting it, and I got the feeling he was interested in her. I've always thought if you're part of a couple, you spend New Year's Eve together, so I broke it off with him. When my parents heard, they encouraged me to fly to California, and we'd go to the mud baths in Calistoga.

Potters like mud, so off I went. The mud was heavy and not as wonderful as I imagined, but my dear mom had thought up the plan to lift my spirits, and I'll always be grateful to her for that.

We went out a few times after that and it flopped for various reasons. The next summer, I took my kids camping in Idaho. Bears opened coolers outside an RV near our tent and ate marsh mellows. I rented a cabin on a lake, where Jerry stayed as a child with his parents. A bear mauled the trash can by the door, but I slept better with a locked door between us.

Driving back from Idaho, I decided to call Jerry, because he was a nice guy, and I missed talking with him. He picked up right away and invited me to meet him at his boat the following day. Ten years later, my kids were off to college, and my daughter said, "What will you do when we're gone? Won't you be bored?"

I smiled. "I have a lot of things I'm going to do."

I moved in with Jerry, sold my house, and we adopted a rescue dog, who was best man at our wedding. I was diagnosed with breast cancer, and he supported me emotionally during a year of surgeries and treatments, listening to my complaints about side effects. These days, he does the grocery shopping, cleaning, and most of the cooking, leaving me with time to write. It turns out my man-picker was broken, but I ended up with the best one in the end.

3

IN THE BATHTUB

I let out a sigh, sinking down into a bubble bath. The house was quiet. All my worries were gone. I flicked a bubble across the bath and thought about an essay I was writing.

A key jungled in the front door lock. I sat up in the bath, listening. The door swung open, and I heard voices.

It was past nine at night, I stood in the bath, heart thudding, and grabbed a towel, calling out in a loud voice, "Who is there?"

No one answered.

Heavy footsteps thudded up the steps from the sunken living room to the main floor. My heart fluttered. I pulled on a robe and strode out to the hall, holding a toothbrush in my hand as a weapon, coming face to face with a tall man.

His eyes skittered over me, taking in my green

terrycloth robe and damp hair. A woman and man in their late twenties stood behind him. They were wearing sport coats and dark slacks, and they didn't look like burglars. The couple raised their eyebrows and looked around, taking in the home.

I unclenched my hands, realizing this was a realtor who had not called ahead, as requested, and we'd said there would be no showings past eight at night.

He didn't apologize, he just glared at me as if I was in the wrong, and he had every right to parade strangers around my house, which he did. The house was up for sale. What did I expect?

I said, "Please call ahead next time and don't show it after eight at night."

The three invaders poked around, opening cupboards and closet doors, peeking into rooms and soon left. None of them apologized for interrupting my bath or almost walking in on me naked. I guess they thought I'd given up my rights when it was listed for sale. The house, with me clearly in the bathtub, probably didn't allow the couple to muse about their hopes and dreams here. It would difficult to imagine moving in to HER home. You wouldn't want to.

That reminds me of the time I toured a house for sale, and the one red mitten left on a paved walkway in the back gave me a creepy feeling. Entering the daylight basement, I stared at a small child's red tricycle on its side, and hairs on the back of my neck stood on end.

I turned to the real estate agent. "Did a little girl die here?"

Her face turned pale, and her lips trembled.

I cleared my throat. "Was she about four years old?"

She nodded. "Yes, she was that age, and she died."

"I'm sorry, but I can't live in this house. Let's see another place."

For me, the home held onto grief. I wonder if the next buyers felt strange vibes upon moving in. I hope they didn't notice or hear what happened.

Jerry and I almost had that happen after buying a house near the San Juan Islands, Washington. We were pulling weeds when a neighbor came over, introduced himself and said, "I live across the street. Do you know why the house didn't sell for almost a year?"

We shook our heads. "No, why?"

"Well, it's a busy street for one thing," he pointed to a road where just a few cars had gone by in the last hour. Later, I learned he was right about that. On some Sundays, a steady stream of car club members drive by. One time, a line of Porches backed up a quarter mile.

He continued, "Two people died there under suspicious circumstances is why."

I gulped and glanced at Jerry, who raised his eyebrows. I hoped we wouldn't tromp inside and discover we didn't like the vibes of our new place. From the sound of it, we might have made a horrible mistake, buying a home no one else wanted.

We said goodbye to the neighbor and finished our yardwork, not wanting to freak out over what he told us. When the weeds were tossed in the green yard waste bin, we took off our gardening gloves and stepped in the house.

I stood in the room where the neighbor said the first owners died. Their bodies were laid out, side by side, but their little dog was alive. A trickle of blood came out of the woman's mouth.

The owners who died came from Las Vegas and built the place. Police said the furnace gave off carbon monoxide and killed them. They found over two-hundred-thousand-dollars in cash in the study, stuffed in plastic trash cans. My husband believes they stole the money from the mob, and they were killed to make a point to others.

Standing in the room where two people were found dead, I didn't feel a strange sensation, and neither did Jerry. We're happy in our not-haunted house, where deer walk on the roof. Cayenne pepper, coyote urine and coffee grounds didn't deter the deer, but sparkling streamers hanging from wires seem to be causing deer detours.

The story about our house and the couple from Vegas with cash influenced my heist thriller, *The Thieves*, if you'd like to check it out.

4

CLOUD COVER

Low gray clouds hung over Seattle for ninety days. People shrugged at first, but then, one by one, we become irritated, down in the dumps, and edgy and angry about the unending dull streak of plain, blah gray weather, repeating itself day after day.

Jerry grumbled, "When's the sun going to shine? I can't take much more of this."

"It's like there's a lid over the city," I said. "It's getting to me. I can't stand it."

His gray blue eyes filled with regret. "We should've gone to see the sun in early January, like we used to. At least then, we would've had a break. Why didn't we do that?"

"I don't know, but we're stuck with it now."

Office mates mentioned it in passing. We counted off

the number of days of continuous low-hanging gray cloudy days. We hadn't seen the sun in forever, it felt like.

Meetings were shorter. Coffee wasn't enough to revive us. Some slept longer, going to bed at eight or nine and rising at six or seven. If economists would have examined the city's productivity during that time, I'm sure they'd have seen a slump.

Finally, one day the sun broke through the clouds, in what Seattle weather forecasters call "sun breaks." Blood pressures went down. Shoulders relaxed. Projects and research papers were completed. People smiled again and life carried on.

At our house in North Seattle, there was no more talk of flying to see the sun. We could do that here and hop on our boat, smiling and laughing and toasting to our good fortune of living in the Pacific Northwest. We were fine, we were wonderful, and we didn't need to leave town to take a vacation. Until the next year, when gray days hit.

We never matched that record, as far as I heard, of ninety consecutive gray days of low-hanging clouds hovering over Seattle. Every now and then, Jerry or I will bring up the subject when we're walking the dog in the rain and complaining about being wet.

One will say, "Remember those ninety straight days of gray low-hanging clouds?"

"Yeah," the other will say, "that was awful."

When the Seattle Mariners play in town, the weather

gods almost always make the sun shine during broadcasts. But don't believe what you see on television, because it's a trick. If you lived here, you'd know there are certain days, weeks and months when you glance outside, shake your head and curl up with a book, biding your time until the sun once again breaks through the clouds.

5

WRITTEN OUT OF TWO WILLS

I have been written out of two wills. For all I know, my name has been struck from more, and I just don't know about them. When I was in college and living in Eugene, Oregon, a document came in the mail from a bank in Detroit. I slit open the brown envelope and pulled out pages mentioning my maternal grandmother's will and showing the names and addresses of beneficiaries.

I glanced at the pages, tossed them in the trash and went on my way, bicycling to my graveyard shift as a nurse's aide in a white dress and white shoes. A police officer gave me a ticket for exceeding the speed limit at ten at night when few cars were out.

The wheels of time turned, and the documents mentioning my grandmother's will stopped coming, but I shrugged it off. I was in my early forties, and one day at work, the phone rang, and I picked it up.

My mother, who never called me at work, said in a tight voice, "Your grandmother died. It was such a shock. She keeled over at the breakfast table and couldn't be revived. We just didn't expect it."

I hung up and burst into tears for my grandmother, who almost made it to one-hundred-years-old. I hurried into the bathroom and sobbed. The grandmother who had doled out peppermint patties to my grade school friends when we rang the door after school and then shooed us out the door, telling me never to come over unless calling first, had passed away. It shouldn't have hit us so hard, but it did.

Life went on, I flew back with my brother John to Detroit, where I rode in first class, using frequent flyer miles, and he was in coach. I gave him the free newspaper, handing it over with a grin, acting my part as the impish youngest sibling. I bet I was a difficult younger sister. In fact, I'm sure of it, because one day I drove a fork into my brother John's cheek during a card game. He ran into the kitchen, where my mother was washing dishes, and he whined, pointing to the fork dangling from his cheek. He said something like, "Look what Susan did."

But Mom just shrugged and said, "You probably deserved it."

The scene is so vivid that I included a fictional version of it in my thriller, *The Cold Night*, where devious Dusty tells the tale at Christmas Eve dinner. Complex family dynamics are fascinating, and our family had our share of it, like when I broke a door in a home where we were staying in Florida on vacation.

My older twin brothers were interested in the same girl down the beach, and tensions were growing. I could feel it in the air. I threw a temper tantrum as a ten-year-old and slammed the sliding door closed, cracking the glass. I cringe now, thinking about it. To make it even worse, my parents watched their pennies, and the home was owned by a minister friend. Imagine the shame of having a belligerent young daughter break a huge glass door. Sorry, Mom and Dad.

After the memorial service, life went on. I didn't think about the will until I received a bright red flyer from a non-profit in San Francisco. "Help us match Liz and Ed's generous gift of $32,000 (or some amount like that). Donate today!"

I squinted and read the words a second time. Liz and Ed, Liz and Ed sounded familiar. My jaw dropped. My penny-wise parents had donated a bundle to the charity.

I tossed the paper in the trash and walked out. I called my mother and she confirmed in an upbeat voice that they'd given the money to a cause that needed it.

"Did the money come from Gago? Is her estate settled now?"

"Yes, that's right."

I sighed and drove my older car that smelled from a

rat crawling under the hood and dying. My kids wore used clothes from thrift stores. We were eating pancakes and scrambled eggs for dinner. Money was tight each month as a single mother.

Later, when I saw her next, Mom mentioned how my parents had helped two other charities with gifts of the same magnitude. Mom flashed a wide smile, and I swallowed hard. I didn't want to sound greedy, but I had to ask. "The grandchildren were in the will before. Did it change?"

She shrugged. "I suppose so. I'm not sure."

"If it did," I pushed on, "it might be nice if you gave a bit of money to my brothers and me, as well as the charities you mentioned."

Her eyes narrowed. "It's my choice, and I don't have to do anything I don't want to."

She changed the subject and that was the end of it until I happened to talk to my aunt, who told me the will had been changed to leave out the grandchildren. My grandmother's intent, my aunt said, was that each sister would give to their children, as had been previously indicated.

The other will I was eliminated from is a shorter story. An artist friend, Monica, called me one day. "Did you know you were cut out of Axel's will?"

I cocked my head. "No, what are you talking about?"

In a hushed voice, she said, "I saw it. I was sent a letter with the names of people who got money from his will, but your name was crossed out in black marker before they copied it. I could still see it."

I said, "That's so strange. I wonder who did it. Thanks for telling me."

A month later, I held a pottery show in my home, and Axel's widow stopped by. She bought pottery and paid me the exact amount that I would have received from her husband's will, before someone crossed out my name.

6

STRETCH

"Make yourself taller," my dad said. "Stand up and straighten your back. Stretch."

My father wanted me to be a stewardess, as we called them back then, to get free flights for family members. But I only grew to five-feet-two-inches, not the required five-foot-three height. Oddly, he didn't mention wanting to fly to specific places until he was in his seventies, when every six months or so, he'd lean forward, blink his brown eyes, and mention to my mom how great it would be if they took one of those river cruises in Europe. He'd say, "Wouldn't it be fun?"

"Maybe later, when I have time," Mom would say.

I asked my mom last week why they never went on a European river cruise. Our friends love those trips and go every six months. Mom said, "I thought we did the same thing, but not on a cruise. I don't think it mattered that much to him."

After my grandmother passed away and money was doled out to her daughters, my parents began to hold mandatory family reunions, where we hunkered down under one roof for a week each summer. Siblings took turns cooking dinner for the group. At the time, I was making thirty-six thousand dollars a year at my job, which was not enough, and my kids qualified for the free lunch program at school. I was too prideful to mention my money shortage, and one evening when it was my night to cook, I made a hearty Ribollita Tuscan bean vegetable stew, like I'd eaten in a Florence café. My sister-in-law asked for my recipe, which I made up, so it must have passed the palate test.

Another year we stayed on Hood Canal in Washington State, and my parents and brothers with their wives stayed in separate bedrooms. Being single, I was assigned to sleep out back with the kids in bunk beds. I soon slipped out to the front deck to sleep under the stars.

Thunder rumbled, coming closer. A flash of lightning zapped across the dark July night sky, and I flinched inside a sleeping bag on a chaise lounge. Rain fell on the wood deck, smacking leaves in nearby trees.

On a noisy, rain-filled night, thunder growled, and lightning lit up the sky. I realized I wanted to spend my vacation time exploring new places with my children. But the next spring, I learned I'd be laid off, due to a buyout and redundancy. Tears streamed down my cheeks as I drove to a Seattle Public Schools administration building to register my kids for middle school.

A man at the counter said, "Is something wrong? You look upset. Everything all right?"

I wiped my eyes. "I just learned I'm losing my job."

"That's rough. Sorry to hear it. I can see why you're upset."

Four months later, I landed a position in Corporate Communications and Investor Relations at another Seattle company, where brilliant minds developed potential treatments for lupus, hepatitis C, cancer and other diseases and conditions. When I had accrued three weeks of vacation and had enough frequent flyer miles to take my twins to Europe, I called the airlines to book flights. The only place we could go was London, according to the woman on the line. I didn't have enough miles to go to Tokyo, Kyoto, or Rome. She found three mileage plan seats on a plane to London in August.

I told my mother about my much-anticipated upcoming marvelous trip, and she said, "But that's when we'll have the family reunion. You'll miss it."

I shrugged on my end of the phone line. "That's the only time we could go. It was difficult to get three seats on the same plane during summer."

We explored London, Bath and Avebury's henge and stone circles, where elderly tourists wandered around holding dowsing rods. In a Cotswold village, my aggrieved eleven-year-olds declared themselves utterly bored, and I strode happily along a public footpath past fields to a pub and enjoyed a brew and the hum of adult conversation. We took a train north to Edinburgh, saw the Fringe Festival and toured Rosslyn Chapel.

When we returned home, I learned the family reunion had not gone well, and the event was never repeated. You might wonder why, but that's not my story to tell, because I wasn't there.

7

DATING

So there I was, a single mom interested in dating after being divorced for a year. I knew I was incendiary material, and anyone I grew close to might burst into flames from proximity to my unsettled issues and baggage. But that didn't stop me from checking out the field.

Feel free to sip a glass of wine and chuckle at my mistakes, I'll bare my soul and share a few details about the oddballs this stranger met.

An eye doctor's eyes filled with tears when we met at a coffee shop near Golden Gardens Park in Seattle. If you visit Seattle, where I lived for many years, you must stop at this park and stand on the sandy beach, inhaling salt air. You can play beach volleyball or wade in frigid water. At night, sit by a bonfire (if you reserve one first), strum a guitar and look west, watching boats come and go from

Shilshole Marina. He hadn't gotten over his recent divorce.

A poet and painter with two young kids lived on a sailboat and sent a poem. He was looking for a mother to his children and would I join them and work to support them? We could all fit in his twenty-eight-foot-long sailboat. There were a few things wrong with his plan, so he was definitely out. When I happened to mention the poet/painter's name where I worked, a man frowned. "He was in my fraternity and never paid his dues. He offered paintings in exchange for payment, and I heard he went to get his paintings back. If I were you, I wouldn't go near him." The painter-poet was out.

After that, I was ready for a refreshing change. A man wrote that he was an artist and photographer. I nodded when I read his message and replied, setting up a meeting at a Starbuck's by Green Lake. My plan was to get in and get out fast if I got weird vibes.

A man with glasses waved from a table, and I smiled and sat down. He was ten years older than he'd said, but I told myself to keep an open mind. Maybe the effort of creating art drained and strained him, so he looks older than he is.

He tapped a long fingernail on the table. Before we could make small talk, he pulled out a portfolio and set it down, staring at me. He forced a wide smile, and his teeth were stained brown. I noticed that his medium-long lanky hair looked like it needed a wash.

I swallowed and my throat was dry, but I was not going to get up and order a cup of tea. Alarms bells were ringing in my head. My instincts were telling me to run. His gaze was intense as he unzipped the portfolio.

He opened it and gestured to the photographs. "This is my work. I wanted you to see it right off, to get your opinions and see if you like it."

I stood and walked around the table for a better view and to provide a springboard for scooting out of there. I took in the Polaroid photos of women naked from the waist up, each looking disgruntled at their state of undress, or with the photographer, or both.

I cleared my throat. "Gosh, that's a lot of photos. See you later."

He turned and squinted at me in an aggressive manner. "But do you like them?"

"Got to go," I said, moving to the exit.

He frowned and slapped his thighs with his hands. "But we only just met."

"Something came up."

I bolted out the door and ran to my car, jumping in and driving away to my home in North Seattle.

That story reminds me of a strange thing that happened when I was pregnant with twins. A man was writing letters to mothers of twins and triplets, who were members of Mothers of Multiples, asking for naked photographs taken while we were pregnant for a research project he was conducting. I didn't write him back.

8

LITTLE RED WAGON

My ninety-three-year-old parents want to stay in their home, north of the Golden Gate Bridge. But time rages against us. My father is on the verge of needing to use a wheelchair, a physician says. His mind is crisp, but his body is failing. My mother is physically strong but has an unreliable memory. Like the navigator and the skipper of a ship, they need each other to ply the waters of life.

Last year, my mother suggested building a tiny home in their back yard for me to live in and take care of them. She'd forgotten about my husband and the life we have with our rescue dog and friends two states north.

"We like where we live," I said, thinking of my brothers who reside in Washington State. "Move north. You'll be close to all of us."

She wrinkled her nose. "We don't like the weather up there."

My husband, Jerry, and I live in a small working waterfront town two hours north of Seattle near the San Juan Islands. Our neighborhood sits on a knob of rock near downtown Anacortes where everyone is named Mary, Kathy, Bob, Bill or Jim, retired baby boomers. I can tell time by looking out the kitchen window. Lyn goes by at seven-thirty each morning, wearing a white blouse or a white down vest. At eight, Mary and David leave their house across the street for a walk. Routine offers a comforting beat to my days.

I flew south last year to help organize my parents' paperwork, at their request, to suggest they move to a retirement center and discuss their fire evacuation route. I tackled the easy task first and, over breakfast, asked where they'd go if a fire swept down. The fire danger zone is a half-mile away, where homeowners can't get fire insurance.

"Not north," my dad said, "that'd be heading into fire territory."

My mom said, "Not east. The bridge would be packed with people."

If a fire headed their way, they decided to drive to the community center.

But the next morning, my mom took me aside. "I think what I need for evacuation in case of fire is a little red wagon."

I tilted my head. "Why do you want a red wagon?"

"I'll have your dad sit in it, and I'll pull him to the community center. I don't think I could pull him very far though, just a block."

I took a deep, calming breath. "The car would be better. Drive to the community center, like you said yesterday."

Later that morning, I moved on to tackling their mountains of paperwork, where they'd asked for my help. Standing in the study doorway, my jaw dropped open. A sea of paperwork covered my dad's computer desk and a rolling file on the right. Stacks of paper squatted on the floor and covered a card table. Piles of paperwork on my mom and dad's desks that unsettled me on my last visit had grown two inches taller. I wondered how they could find anything.

Gesturing to the paperwork, I said to my dad, "This mess doesn't look like you."

"I don't know where to start," he said with tears in his eyes.

With my father's permission, I started on the right side of his desk and pulled out Consumer Reports, asking how long he wanted to keep the magazines. My mom carried Consumer Reports from 2011 through 2017 to the recycle bin, and we exchanged smiles.

Sitting cross-legged on the floor, I handed him papers. "Recycle, keep or shred?"

Over three and a half hours, a spot on the wood floor

opened up. I filed invoices, utility bills and Visa statements at his direction. All of a sudden, I understood what
started his paperwork tornado. He'd been hospitalized in
2019. After that, papers piled up.

We turned to the card table, while Mom heated
salmon and fish tacos for dinner.

By the time my mom said, "Dinner is served," my dad
had cleared a one-foot square of the green felt card table.
Later, as we cleared the dinner dishes, my dad hugged me
and thanked me for my help.

I had one last task. My father is on the verge of
needing to use a wheelchair, but the doorways in my
parents' home aren't wheelchair accessible. Moving to a
retirement home a half-mile away, I reasoned, would
simplify their lives, with fewer bills to pay and meals
prepared. Nursing care was available and the rooms
accommodated wheelchairs. My paternal grandmother
lived there and liked it. The week before, a physician
suggested they move to a retirement community and
specifically recommended The Redwoods. But even
though a doctor recommended it, the subject was a deli-
cate one.

"What do you think of moving to the Redwoods," I
said, "or another retirement place? You wouldn't have to
maintain a house or pay so many bills. It'd be easier on
you."

My mom frowned. "I'd miss my garden."

"We're staying here," my dad said.

On a recent visit, I again broached the topic of moving to the local retirement center because my dad's ability to walk is declining. My mother agreed to take a tour.

In the Redwoods' courtyard, chaise lounges, sun umbrellas and patio tables made it look like a resort. Garden plots were available. Activities included Tai Chi, yoga, meditation, book groups, political activist meetings and more. The restaurant offered several main courses for lunch and dinner. Take out was available. Residents smiled when they saw us. We left with a packet of information and two applications.

At three in the afternoon at my parents' dining room table as sunlight streamed in, I said, "You could put in an application in case something happens and you can't stay in your home. We don't know what the future will bring. This would be a backup option."

"Not right away though," my mom said.

"We'd tell them in six to nine months or more," I said. "You don't have to move if you submit an application. It's a fallback plan."

My dad said, "We'd need two toilets."

I nodded. "You'd ask for a double studio. They have two toilets."

"Okay," my mom said with a smile. "Let's do it."

An hour later, my husband and I walked the completed applications with a deposit to the retirement center and dropped the envelope off.

We were due the next morning at six o'clock to slip out

and drive home. But as Jerry and I tiptoed out of the back room, a voice came from the dark living room.

"You can turn the light on," my mom said.

She appeared in the kitchen, red-eyed with wild white hair.

"I couldn't sleep," she said. "Why did we apply? We can't live there. I'm not moving into that small space."

"It's just an option," I said, my heart beating fast, ambushed on our way out the door. "They might not have an opening for the type of place you wanted."

"It's a door that might open," my husband said, "but you don't have to walk through it."

We hopped in the car and left my parents to ponder their future as we drove north, eager to get home where deer walk on the roof of our berm-like house and otters come up the street to eat koi in a neighbor's pond. When I called my parents the next day, my mother's mood had changed. She was positive about having the option to move someday to the Redwoods. Two days later, she was against it.

My parents aren't alone in their wanting to age in place. An AARP Home and Community Preferences 2021 survey showed seventy-seven percent of those age fifty and older want to remain in their homes. A greater number of older households will create a pressing need for supportive services according to the Harvard Joint Center for Housing Studies' The State of the Nation's Housing 2022 report.

We don't know what the future holds and our story is unfinished. But I'm trying to prepare and help my parents evaluate their choices, in case their needs change. My husband and I picked out a retirement community if we have to leave our home. We'd rather finish out our days in our house, but it might not be possible. If we must move to a retirement home or nursing facility, we can only hope to find a human connection in a sea of change.

I was flying home from visiting my parents and thinking about the freedom to live where you want and to die in your home. I looked out the plane window at green trees covering hillsides once burned from Mt. St. Helens' mighty blast of an eruption. A spirited man named Harry R. Truman was a prospector and inn-keeper who defied evacuation orders and refused to leave his home near Mt. St. Helens before the mountain blew. When Mt. St. Helens exploded in 1980, he died in the blast. But he was home, where he wanted to be.

The ash-clogged river is now blue, sparkling in the sun, and showing signs of renewal. Like Harry R. Truman, my parents and my husband and I would like to finish our lives in familiar surroundings. Whether our bodies and bank accounts will cooperate remains to be seen.

Next up is Book 6, *Phone Call*, in the *Strangers on a Train Series*.

PHONE CALL

TRUE STRANGE TALES

1

PHONE CALL

My phone rang Friday afternoon with a call from an Unknown Caller, and I almost didn't answer it, but I did. "Hello?"

"This is Joyce, the nurse practitioner at your mother's primary care office. We spoke last week."

"Yes. Thanks for calling."

"I wanted to catch you before you flew back to Seattle. I checked, and we have her final biopsy results."

We'd been waiting for the results for seventeen long days. I said in a low voice, "What did it show?"

"I'm sorry to say, we have confirmation she has cancer."

We said goodbye, and I went to have a conversation with my mother that we thought we'd never have. Sipping tea, we talked about end-of-life decisions and what she wanted. We continued the conversation over a dinner of leftover fish tacos.

Mom said, "You're willing to talk about death, and I guess it's because you had cancer."

I nodded. "Also, I worked in nursing homes, hospitals and people's houses with sick and dying people when you cut me off financially."

She pursed her lips and suggested we not revisit negatives from the past.

Life is confusing and very strange, because you wouldn't think I'd be helping my mother after my parents refused to acknowledge me or have a relationship for several years. But I'm treating her with kindness because I'd like my kids to do that when I'm older. If I ignored her calls and emails, I'd have more time on my hands but less self-respect.

2

LEGS LIKE JELLO

One day, I called my mom and we chatted. When I asked how my father was doing, she mentioned he was in the hospital. I bit my lip. "He's in the hospital? Why didn't you call me and tell me?"

"His legs were like Jello. He couldn't stand up, so the neighbor helped me get him in the car, and I drove to the emergency room."

"Call 911 next time. And let me know right away. When did this happen? This morning?"

"No, four days ago."

"He's been in the hospital for four days and you didn't tell me?"

"Well, I've been busy. I've been doing things."

I hung up, called the hospital and spoke with the charge nurse. She said my father had acute renal failure.

When I told Mom his diagnosis, she said, "How do you know that?"

"I spoke with the charge nurse, and she told me."

"Well, all I know is his legs were like Jello."

I called my dad in his hospital room, and he said in a choked-up voice, "I'm alone here. Your mother hardly ever comes to see me."

I blew out a breath, recalling how my husband rarely left my side when I was in the hospital. "I'm sorry you're going through that. I'm flying down, and I'll be there when you're discharged."

Later, I asked my mother if she had avoided the hospital and seeing Dad because of what her father went through. It's weird to think about now, but in the 1960's, my grandfather was in the hospital for many months with prostate cancer, and that's where he passed away. For some, a hospital isn't a place to heal and get help, but where one goes to die.

3

___

GET BACK TO THE DORMS

I flew out to Eugene to start at a new college, and my parents shipped my yellow bicycle by train. I slid into a seat at an orientation session being held for transfer students and soon noticed a guy with curly brown hair in front who raised his hand and asked questions. We bumped into each other in the student union, where the movie *Animal House* was later filmed, and we talked.

Bicycling in the Oregon rain, with every turn of the pedals, I wanted to break away and explore what I'd missed by growing up in a strict Christian household. I became friends with the young man with curly brown hair, and a month later, I moved in with him. His nickname was "Easy" for his easy-going nature and how he liked to laugh.

My parents had seen the movie *Nashville*, and they were sure my new boyfriend had that nickname because of his many romantic relationships, although that wasn't the case. Mom sent me a handwritten letter with lots of underlining, telling me I was living in sin and to "get back to the dorms where you belong."

The letter smelled like judgement and reeked of the lifestyle I left behind when I flew out to the West Coast. I was learning to make my own choices and having fun cooking and living in a little house not far from campus.

My mother sent a second letter saying if I didn't move back to the dorms where I belonged, they'd cut me off financially. The letter had a mean, strident, angry tone, so much so that the curly-haired man still remembers it and I do too. I think I tossed it in the trash with the vegetable peelings.

My folks had paid for the first quarter's tuition, but that flew by, and I was on my own. For the rest of my undergraduate education, I worked graveyard shifts as a certified nurse's aide, filling in at hospitals, nursing homes and in people's houses. The best job I had was at the Student Health Center on campus, where students who were ill could stay overnight. Wiping up vomit from drunk students was disgusting, but at around four in the morning, a heavenly scent of homemade cinnamon rolls made with butter and brown sugar wafted up from the kitchen, filling the halls.

I made friends with a nurse on duty, who had a fondness for chocolate pudding pies. We invited her and her boyfriend over for dinner with another couple, and I made the mistake of heating water for spaghetti in a big black canning pot. It seemed like it took over an hour for the water to boil, and our guests were growing hungry and glassy-eyed. But we finally did eat, sitting on the floor around a brown tablecloth and eating off second-hand plates from Goodwill.

We became best friends with the couple who lived next door, and we got puppies at the same time. A banjo-playing friend moved into an apartment across the parking lot, and when I baked bread, friends would appear at the back door, knocking and asking for a slice. We'd cut the loaf, add a thick layer of butter to each piece and moan at the mouth-watering flavor. All was right with the world.

Another friend revealed he'd been a bank robber, and we shrugged. He said he'd used a cap gun, so it wasn't really a big deal. He shouldn't have been charged, and we all nodded.

But the ones with the dog next door started to rebuff friends, insulting them and sending them away one by one. The husband called me "petty," and said we couldn't be friends anymore or hang out as couples. My boyfriend was cut off a few weeks later for a perceived personality defective trait. It turns out the accuser carried the burden of being venomously angry at his father for making him ride a tractor and plow fields at a young age, ruining his hearing, among other offenses.

Our band of bonded forever friends broke up, and we

moved to Springfield, across the river, which turned out to be a serious error in judgement, because we only had bicycles for commuting, and it was a long ways. I knew we'd made a mistake two months in, riding at night in a white dress to a hospital gig, where I was filling in for a shift. I scraped together all my money I'd saved from waitressing when I graduated early from high school. I hadn't touched it and thought I'd take a backpacking trip to Europe that I'd always dreamed about.

Instead of flying off to see foreign sights, I bought a used 1962 VW camper bus. We were set. We camped on the Oregon Coast during Spring Break with our dog. Listening to rain patter on the roof of the camper van at a state park, eating gingerbread at a café, I smiled at the young man with curly hair and knew I'd made a good choice, by picking him over my parents.

4

WORK WITH MY FATHER

My dad took me to hardware stores on Saturdays. Mom took me to high school, church, shopping and to see my friends. One day, long before take your child to work day, I hopped in the car with my dad and we went to his work. I wore knee length boots with fringe at the top, a rust-colored suede skirt and a blue and yellow striped turtleneck. Clothes were very important to me in high school, so I remember what I wore.

My dad had talked at the dinner table about the price of sugar going up, and how he had made a mistake and bought sugar at what turned out to be the peak price. He had been admonished at work for buying two or three railcar loads of sugar and not foreseeing the future.

My father was a pharmacist who worked for Parke-Davis, a pharmaceutical company, and he worked as Vice

President of Purchasing. I remember cowering in a corner of the dining room when I was sick, and he came at me with a spoon holding a new flavor of cherry cough syrup being tested at work. It tasted awful, the kind of sweet, cloying taste that sticks to the back of your throat, even after you drink a glass of water.

If we had a sore throat, we were told to gargle with Listerine, another product from my dad's company. A bee sting? Benadryl was just the thing to take.

Anyway, there I was going into downtown Detroit with my dad and walking into the office building by the Detroit River. My older brothers and I heard our dad's work stories over the dinner table, before he sat by the stereo and did his "homework" to catch up on reading.

That day at his work, we ate lunch in the executive lounge, if I recall right. It was pretty fancy and looked out over the river, where freights glided by on their way to the Great Lakes. Gordon Lightfoot sang about the wreck of the Edmund Fitzgerald, and that ill-fated ship would have passed my father's office building on the way north, before the storm struck, sinking the ship.

Many years later, it turned out my listening to my dad talk about his job was beneficial when I was a newly divorced single mom of five-year-olds needing a job. (Side note: Our daughter nearly died at birth and had a chronic illness, which can stress a marriage. She had been without oxygen for ten minutes and had a zero Apgar score out of a possible score of ten. A pediatrician at Children's

Hospital in Seattle told us she likely wouldn't make it a day or two, and if she did, she wouldn't be able to walk or feed herself or talk. When she survived and was released from the hospital, I turned into the Germ Patrol and was super stressed about protecting her health. Doctors put our family in quarantine for the first two years, so she wouldn't contract RSV, a deadly respiratory virus. I'm sure I wasn't pleasant to live with, being on edge and sleep deprived, and the marriage broke apart.)

I applied at a temp agency for a position, and they were stunned at my typing speed and floored by the number of mistakes I made. They sent me for an interview at a biotechnology company for a summer position to assist with their Wall Street analyst meeting.

I was hired and it turned out I was comfortable in that environment, where they were developing drugs to help patients with cancer, inflammation and other diseases. Oddly, after ten years of being a potter and selling at art fairs, I was well-suited to assist with an event and help with logistics, like lining up limos to take executives and Wall Street analysts to dinners at restaurants. Because I grew up around wealthy people, although that description didn't fit our family, I was comfortable talking to analysts who controlled millions and billions of dollars in their funds. They're people, just like the rest of us.

5

THE GUITAR

I was learning to play guitar when I was about fourteen. A photo shows me half-smiling and turning away from the camera, in part because of my acne-ridden face. I hate photos being taken of me to this day, but I'm working on being relaxed in front of the camera. It's never too late to learn life skills.

In the photo, I'm wearing a red crew-neck sweater and a white blouse, sitting on the back steps of our brick house by a white picket fence, strumming a guitar. I felt the need to go inside, maybe to call a friend and gossip, or get a drink of water, so I set the guitar against the brick wall of the house.

The white fence probably looked on, warning, "Don't do that."

But I didn't listen, because I was young. Possessions

could be fixed or replaced. I was going to live forever, and so would everyone in my family. But that was before what I know now.

I was in the kitchen, perhaps drinking orange High-C, and I heard a cry of despair from outside. My mother sounded upset, so I rushed out the back door and stopped in my tracks. She held the mangled neck of the guitar in her hands, cradling it and frowning.

She said in a tight voice, "It's broken. How did this happen?"

The music stopped that day, and I never played again. The poor guitar was broken in two parts at the neck. It must have blown over in the wind. And it was all my fault.

She didn't wash my mouth out with lava soap, as she had two times before when I yelled swear words. She didn't spank me with a hairbrush, making me lean over her knee, as she had when I was younger, until one day I fought back, jumping up and clenching my fists, saying she couldn't do that. Her eyes grew wide, perhaps realizing I was her size, and that put an end to what she says was Dr. Spock's advice to spank kids to teach them to behave.

Mom's vast disappointment in me was evident in her deep sighs as we walked into the house. She grasped the guitar and was silent. I swallowed, and my throat was dry. The somber mood continued, and a pall was cast over the house by my wrong-doing.

I felt bad but shrugged it off with the carelessness of an adolescent. One of my brothers recently asked about the guitar. He wanted to play it, but it was gone. I don't recall what happened to it.

Speaking of possessions, I was recently at her home helping her. We went out for happy hour at a nearby restaurant, eating delicious shrimp tacos and drinking beer, and the owner recognized my extroverted, smiling mother, giving us a discount. In a strangled hoarse voice, she said thank you.

We'd talked about giving some unused items away, so one afternoon, I opened a closet and pulled out an air horn my parents used when they lived on boat years ago. Grasping the heavy metal horn in my hand, I went into the dining room.

The sun shone on the flower garden. She glanced up and smiled, and I held up the chrome horn. "How about we give this away?"

She frowned. "Oh, no, we can't do that."

I cocked my head. "You want to keep this?"

She nodded. "Definitely, yes, we can't give that away. It's useful."

I suppressed a groan. "How about giving it to a family member?"

"No, absolutely not. I want to keep it."

I sighed and returned to the closet, setting down the air horn that deserved a better life, where it would be used by boaters. Sliding the closet door closed, I let go of the notion that Mom would part with her possessions. This was the wrong time to ask. We had bigger things to focus our attention on, like medication for her increasing pain. Let go and move on and give me the strength, I thought, glancing around the two-bedroom house packed with possessions, like a clay pharmacist figurine.

Don't bother, I told myself. Focus on breathing slowly and relaxing. Don't try to control minutia. Things in her house that look like clutter matter to her, and she wants to keep them. Respect that and her final wishes. Focus on what matters most.

I must find a way to float through this confusing ending time, giving her love and surviving a tidal wave sweeping us under each day, and we gasp, swimming to shore. I want to be the daughter she needs during this difficult time, but also manage to be a good wife and the dog owner Abby deserves.

I'm back home now, writing this, and Abby's head rests on my left knee. The gas fireplace is off, and the morning is underway, with my husband in the shower listening to sports radio at full volume. Bringing myself back from worries about my mother, I ponder the day ahead. What do I want to do with my time? I'm retired, where every week has six Saturdays and one Sunday.

I'll email my mother with an inspiring quote*, finish a library book and tell you a story about the deathbed promise I made to my father. Those final words changed my life, and I wrote a similar scene in my novel of suspense, *Secrets at the Café.*

*Here is the quote from Elizabeth Kubler-Ross: "It's only when we truly know and understand that we have a limited time on earth... we will then begin to live each day to the fullest, as if it was the only one we had."

6

FIREFIGHTERS

My mother called one Thursday afternoon and said in a hushed voice, "I think this is it. He took three of those vials."

I winced. "Oh, no." My dad was in hospice, and this sounded final. I was three states away.

She said, "He told me thanks for being my friend."

"That is so sweet." I glanced at my husband, who was listening, sitting across from me at the kitchen island. My father didn't normally talk like that. Maybe this was the end.

"I called hospice to let them know," she said, sounding remarkably coherent and composed, given the circumstances.

"Okay, let me know what they say."

I hung up, and Jerry said, "You'd better go."

My brain froze. My fingers hovered over the laptop

keyboard. I knew I wanted to see what flights were available, but I was suddenly light-headed. It was difficult to breathe.

"Slow down," he said. "Take a moment. It can wait until you collect your thoughts."

"But I need to book a flight now."

I logged on to my favorite airline's website, but my mind went blank. I couldn't concentrate. I leaned against the counter and let out a long sigh. Inhaling a deep breath, I drank a glass of water, wiped away a tear and turned my attention to booking a flight.

I tapped on the keyboard. "There's only one seat left on the one o'clock flight tomorrow. I'll take that." My jaw dropped. "It's gone. Someone just took it."

Searching for earlier flights, there was one seat left on the six in the morning flight out of Everett, north of Seattle. I booked it. I looked up, blinking back tears, because although I'd known this day would come, I wasn't ready. I blew out a breath and said to Jerry, "I got the last seat on the six o'clock flight."

His eyes opened wide. "Six in the evening?"

"No, the first flight in the morning. We'll leave here at three-thirty tomorrow morning."

We groaned at the early departure time and embraced each other. He is an unwanted expert in dying, because his parents have passed away. Mine were breakers of statistical averages, bringing up the longevity curve. Dad bragged after doctor visits that the staff said he looked young, as if he was in his seventies, when he was ninety-three. He believed his comb-over created a youthful appearance.

I inherited the genes for looking younger, which worked against me when a client at a consulting firm thought I was in high school, but I had graduated from college two years before. My youthful looks vanished after a year of cancer treatments, in what a friend called "the longest year of our lives." But as tough as that time was, cancer made me look ahead and create a vision for the rest of my life.

But back to my dad. Tears streamed down my cheeks at Paine Field in Everett and as I boarded the plane. It was one of those moments where you know you're in touch with the big, important part of life, standing on the edge of death and grieving.

I flew into San Francisco, took an Uber north and used my key to let myself in the house. The place was quiet. My dad was in bed and couldn't talk or open his eyes. I spoke with my mom and told him I loved him. I asked him to blink if he wanted jazz music put on. His right eye blinked, but the left one didn't move.

"Only his right eye blinked," I said, looking at my mother.

She said, "His left eye stopped working."

I took my mom's laptop, signed up for Pandora and picked a jazz music station. When the first busy notes tumbled out, I looked at Dad, who was frowning, and said, "Sorry, that's right, you wanted soft jazz. Hold on."

I changed the station to soft jazz, and his clenched hands relaxed. His facial features softened. A lot happened that day as Mom helped him walk his last mile, reading from a red prayer book from church (I joked later that she had stolen it from church, but she didn't find it funny). A hospice nurse sat with us during the day and into late afternoon, increasing the doses of his medications and adding new ones to relieve his pain.

The firefighters arrived to help Dad sit up in bed, because he was sinking down, despite being propped up on pillows. A quick call was put into the hospital bed company, and the guy came right over, setting up the bed and telling me his life story. It was fascinating, but given what was going on that day, I forgot the details.

The firefighters were to carry my failing, fading father from the marriage bed (used by them for a gazillion years!) to the newly set up hospital bed in the living room. Jazz music was no longer playing. Dad was unresponsive now, and the nurse couldn't administer med's through his mouth, because he couldn't swallow. He was choking on his saliva, which is not the way he'd want to die, and none of us would.

Three fire fighters, one young, one middle-aged and one a bit older, but all beefy and strong, lifted my dad, and I left the small bedroom because it was too crowded.

A neighbor came over to ask what was going on

because she saw the fire truck. Mom spoke to her, and the youngest red-faced firefighter rushed out, waving his hands at me in the living room.

"We lost pulse! DNR?"

I opened my eyes wide. "What?"

"DNR! Does he have a DNR?"

"Yes." I ran to the kitchen, pulled the POLST form with the Do Not Resuscitate order off the refrigerator, where we'd placed it five years before, and handed it to him.

"Got it," he called, racing into the bedroom.

The middle-aged man with defined biceps said, "Pulse came back on its own. We'd better leave him be and not move him. Got any more pillows to prop up his head?"

We gathered pillows, and the fire fighters stood on the bed, pulling Dad's frail body up higher in the bed, moving him gently and firmly, with respect.

The younger flushed faced man turned to me, saying in a low voice, "What's wrong with him?"

I whispered. "He's dying. Today might be his last day."

And it was.

7

DEATHBED PROMISE

On the afternoon of my dad's day of death, as the tax man called it, the firefighters tromped out of the house, leaving my father propped up in bed by many pillows. The hospice nurse had initially said Dad might pass in a few weeks when she arrived before noon, but as the hours ticked on, her forecast grew shorter, to a few days to later today. A new hospice nurse was called to replace the one who had attended to Dad diligently. When she left, she said to me, "It won't be long now."

A new nurse arrived, his curly hair wild, and he looked around with darting eyes, introducing himself. I showed him into the bedroom, where my mother was speaking in soft tones to my father, with her hand resting gently on his shoulder.

The new nurse checked my father, administered

medications and said he had to go. He blew out the front door with a frantic energy. Minutes ticked by, and then an hour.

Mom started to make dinner. It seems like a strange thing to do, to prepare food and plan to eat when your loved one is passing away in the next room. Routine is a life raft we cling to, I suppose, and although Dad was leaving the planet, we were going to go on living.

Pots clanged in the kitchen. Water ran in the sink. A metal spatula scraped on a frying pan. Mom was cooking chicken and broccoli, and she'd done an incredible job helping Dad that day. The hospice nurse said she was amazed at how we focused on my father and didn't bring our baggage to the situation. She said it was clear we wanted to help him leave his body peacefully. Some families are loud and distract from the death, by arguing, weeping loudly and making the event about themselves.

My father had been in severe pain for years, an eleven on a ten scale of pain he told us, and the peripheral neuropathy in his hands and feet shrank his life, and he rarely left the house in his last year. He was ready to go, and our job was to support him.

He'd told me in confidence on a previous visit, leaning forward in his recliner and saying in a soft voice when my mom was out of the room, how he'd been considering driving to Hoover Dam, where the huge magnet would make his pacemaker stop. Or a new iPhone battery held against his heart might have the same effect, to stop his heart. Hospice was a better way, he eventually decided.

Mom hunched over the stove, grim-faced and jaw clenched.

A hunch drew me back to their bedroom, and I tiptoed in stocking feet, standing in the doorway in the house I never lived in. The last hospice nurse said before he left that it wouldn't be long before Dad died. I moved closer to the bed. Was Dad dead?

I sat on the bed by him and watched his chest slightly, slowly rise and fall. I'd heard that people wait to die until they were alone, but he'd had an hour by himself. What was he waiting for? And then I knew with certainty what he wanted to hear.

He'd told me three years before that he had been hanging on and not going into hospice earlier because someone needed to take care of my mother. His eyes filled with tears, and he said, "She couldn't manage on her own."

Looking at Dad in bed, I blew out a breath, put my hands behind my head and rested on Mom's side of the double bed. Side by side, father and daughter, I listened to his ever so faint slow breathing and said, "Dad, I know you're waiting for something before you go. You spoke with your sons, and they said they loved you, and it was okay for you to go. Mom has been here, and I have too, saying our goodbyes."

I waited a beat and continued, "I think you're waiting for me to say I'll take care of Mom after you're gone."

Something about the still silence in the room changed as soon as I uttered those words. His chest didn't move, as if he was waiting for what I'd say next.

"I'll take care of Mom, don't worry. I'll make sure the bills are paid, and she's safe, I'll take care of her. I love you, Dad. You can go now. I love you."

I got up and slipped out of the room into the noisy kitchen, where the stovetop fan whirred. Mom and I sat and ate a few bites. Five minutes after we started eating, I set down my fork and knife. "I'll check on Dad," I said. "I think he passed."

And he had. His chest wasn't rising or falling any longer. I didn't go close to check for a pulse or see if he was breathing, because I felt like my mother might want to do it, and maybe I was afraid to see death right in front of me.

I went into the kitchen and told Mom I thought he'd passed. She got up, went into the bedroom and confirmed it in a calm voice.

We called hospice to report it, and a nurse came an hour later, pronouncing Dad dead. A few hours later, two mortuary workers dressed in black arrived in an unmarked van in the dark of night. One man was tall and thin, the other was short and plump, as if they had popped out of a cartoon show. They zipped my father's husk of a shell into a black body bag and wheeled him on a gurney out of the house.

Mom and I stood at the living room window waving goodbye to Dad, as they loaded him in the back of a van. They drove off, and we closed the window blinds, going to bed. Dad was gone, and a new chapter of our lives had begun.

Next up is Book 7, *Watering Can,* in the *Strangers on a Train Series*.

WATERING CAN

TRUE STRANGE TALES

1

BOWLING

When my twins were in morning preschool, I took one of them out for a special outing each week to bond with my son and daughter separately for a few hours. Some fraternal twins complain about being viewed as a two-pack, not as individuals, and I went so far as to have separate birthday cakes for them on their birthday.

One Friday morning, I pulled my almost five-year-old daughter out of preschool and took her to a bowling alley. Bowling balls rumbled down lanes, classic rock music played in the background, and the aroma of French fries wafted past. A gum-chewing man with thinning hair assigned us a lane where no one was bowling on either side. Other bowlers were in their sixties and seventies with gray hair.

We put on bowling shoes and picked out balls, hefting

them in our hands. We threw mostly gutter balls, but a few wobbled down the wooden lane, knocking down pins. We raised our hands and cheered.

A group farther down roared when someone got a strike, and my gaze flicked away to them. But when I looked back at my daughter, she was slowly walking down the greased lane, holding a bowling ball. She was eight feet from the marked line, moving closer to the pins, and I called for her to come back.

She glanced back at me, the ball fell out of her hands, rolling into the gutter, and her feet flipped out from under her. The music stopped, and the bowling alley suddenly was quiet. People gasped. Bowlers who were about to bowl stood staring at us. No one moved.

Flat on the floor, she crawled on the slick surface toward me, having a tough time making little progress. I ventured out to her, treading with my arms out, as if skating on ice, but I fell, smacking my hip on the hard maple floor and letting out a groan.

She inched forward like a worm wiggling on a wet road, and I swam on the slick surface to where she held out a hand. Grasping her and holding her close, I scooted backwards on my butt. People watched open-mouthed, gaping at what must never happen in a bowling alley.

We made it back to the line one must not cross when throwing a ball and wiped our greasy palms on our pants. The music started, and bowlers bowled, knocking down pins with a clatter and whoops of joy.

We finished our game, and years later, on a fourth-grade field trip, my daughter bowled the best in her group, but she didn't care. She'd had enough of bowling. Looking back, I wonder why I didn't go in the gutter to rescue her, but I lost common sense in the commotion and was struck by myopia in the moment.

2

HOW WAS YOUR DAY

I tromped through the front door of the house on South Beacon Hill in Seattle, threw down my purse and sighed. My curly-haired husband watched me and asked about my day. I groaned and complained about office drama but noticed he was quiet.

"What about you? How was your day?"

He blinked back tears. "We ran out of body bags at the hospital today."

I bit my lower lip.

He continued, "I took a dead person down in the elevator with a white sheet over their body, and other people got on."

My hands flopped down at my sides. "I'm sorry. How awful."

After that, I hope I curtailed my whining about my

work, because dealing with death and dying and disease is much more important than a Senator's grandson reading the Wall Street Journal all day. His job mattered, and mine was a mere speck on the ocean.

3

LEAD DUST

I tromped up the cement steps to the two-bedroom house in Seattle, where the babysitter was watching my two-year-old twins. The front door was closed, the windows shut and no one was playing outside, which was odd on a warm September afternoon. A loud noise next door whirred and buzzed. When I went inside, the babysitter took me aside.

"We're playing inside," she said, wiping her brow, "because something's going on next door. They started sanding and dust was flying everywhere, all over the deck, so we came in until they're finished."

I went out to see the neighbor, who had mentioned this project and told me he'd tell me ahead of time before he sanded the exterior of his house with five layers of old paint. Doctors told us our daughter could not be exposed to dust, and inhaling it might put her in the hospital, because she had so little lung function left. The neighbor turned off the sander and shrugged, saying he might take a few weeks to get the job done.

The babysitter left, and my husband came home and called his parents, asking if we could stay a few weeks until the sanding next door was finished. They invited us over, and I wonder if they regretted that offer, because our children were loud and rambunctious, running through their quiet home.

The sanding continued. I called a government agency, but they arrived to inspect the flying dust when the workers were on lunch break. I took a video of the dust flying, but I was told there were no precedents or state laws that prohibited the pollution. I took swabs of the dust on our deck and other spots, which turned out to have at a high-level of contamination, with parts per million at a level seen in Superfund Sites. I hired an independent lab, and their tests confirmed the high levels of lead in the dust and the soil.

The State of Washington had no laws on the books at that time, like Massachusetts had, requiring containment of work areas when sanding exteriors of houses. A dog a block down died (!) when another house with old paint was sanded, from padding through fouled soil on his property.

We lived with my in-laws, who were in their seventies,

with my bickering, joyous fraternal twins for seven months. The babysitter quit because it took two busses to reach us. Sales at my pottery shop and small art gallery plummeted.

I hired a lead abatement company to come in and remove the contamination, which spread in our house when the furnace kicked on in cooler weather, sucking in outside air and blowing particles all around. Our insurance company decided to cover part of the lead abatement cost.

I spoke with the owners of a day care in a home behind us, because their back yard was also exposed to flying lead dust from sanding down layers of old lead paint, but they shrugged. The one-eyed roofer and his wife has bigger concerns, like raising a grandchild and running a daycare out of their home.

The whole thing riled me up, and I met with four lawyers to make it right. Items in our home were tossed in a dumpster when they couldn't be adequately cleaned, like my husband's boots, and the quilt I took five years to sew, and a Hudson Bay blanket, where I'd embroidered on the corner.

Three lawyers turned me down and said there was no precedent on our state for such a lawsuit. The final and fourth lawyer was eager to take the case on contingency, but then he called and said in a sad voice, "I'm sorry to tell you this, but I can't take the case."

"Why not?"

"The other party is wealthy, and they threatened to sue you. It's not a matter of who is right, but who has the most money. We need to let this go. If your name was Nordstrom, we'd purse this case."

I hung up the phone and gazed at my children playing on a jungle gym in my in-law's daylight basement. Justice wasn't available in our state. I'd have to let it go, but my fingers itched to take a swing at them, the couple who ruined our lives and caused us to spend over one-hundred-thousand-dollars in lead abatement bills, not including the cost of replacing tossed out belongings.

A neighbor told me the neighborhood sided against us. They thought we were crazy and making a big deal out of nothing. It was just dust, and we should have shrugged it off.

I frowned, hearing that, and suggested to my husband that we sell the house when it was lead-abated and certified as cleaned up and a healthy place to live. Over a foot of contaminated dirt was dug up from the yard and tossed in a dumpster, hauled off to a biohazardous waste site. But the neighbors thought we were weird.

I wondered last year about the children at the daycare next door, but we'll never know if or how the dust affected their health and development. Curious about the home-owners who caused the chaos in our small lives, I searched online. The wife of the sander was pregnant and living in the home across the narrow alley while their house was sanded. Online, I found posts by her about having serious health issues, but I don't know if they were connected to the layers of lead dust flying in the air. But it does make me wonder if it all came back to bite them in the end.

4

BROWN COW

A long-legged boy leaned on the counter, sipping a concoction in a tall glass. He looked to be about a year older than me, and I was about eight. My grandmother belonged to a small country club by a lake, and I had been sent to day camp there, where other campers already knew each other. In swimming class, I was told to doggie paddle from one side of the pool to the other.

When I finished swimming, I hopped out and sat on a bar stool, ordering a brown cow with vanilla ice cream and root beer. The older boy beside me spoke with a man behind the counter but not to other campers. I hadn't seen him in activities. He was aloof, as if he was from a distant planet but forced to share gravity on earth with the rest of us.

Years later, a young man introduced himself to me at a

high school cafeteria table. He wore a red and white striped shirt, and his brown eyes exuded warmth, making me feel I met a friend. I figured out he was the stranger who sat beside me after swim class, two outcasts perched on bar stools. He lived there when his parents managed the club.

5

OPERA

In Rome, Italy, I wanted to go to the opera, but my stomach growled with hunger, so I stopped at a mostly empty restaurant and ate delicious pasta. Paying the bill, I left and examined a map as traffic roared by.

Walking down a few blocks, I stopped at a street corner and looked around but couldn't see a sign for the opera. A group of men in white tails stood outside on the sidewalk, and I went over and asked a man in white tails, "Dove opera?"

His eyes lit up, and he smiled, motioning for me to follow him inside. I slipped through a side door and sat down on a hard seat. The man in white tails picked up a trumpet and played, just like my boyfriend did back home. He'd brought me through the musician's entrance to see the second half of *Tosca*, an opera by Puccini.

Music swept over the audience, opera singers belted out beautiful notes, and a chill ran up my spine. I shivered and smiled as goosebumps pricked my flesh, having ended up exactly where I wanted to be.

6

SPECIAL DELIVERY

The crisp smell of fall was in the air, and high school classes in our suburb of Detroit had started. Harry's letter arrived Special Delivery, and I opened it with shaking hands. He was older than I was and lived in a small city in Ontario, two-and-a-half hours away. I looked at the letter but didn't understand the dots and dashes, so I took it to my babysitting job on the next block.

The father greeted me at the door and asked how I was. I said, "My boyfriend sent a letter, but I think it might be in code."

He smiled. "Do you have it with you? I'll take a look. I was in the Navy."

I handed him the letter, and the father read it, rubbing his chin. He gave it back and said, "It's in Morse Code. He said he loves you."

I bit my lip, because I was sixteen, and we met during a difficult summer, where a tragic accident made us all quieter and the voice of death hung heavy in our hearts. Something about the way the father of the kids I was babysitting looked at me gave me the feeling the letter might have said more than he let on.

I wrote Harry back, telling him about classes but didn't say I loved him. He wrote about training to be an electrician and asked me to move to Canada. We could get married. My mouth went dry when I read that. I wasn't ready to take that huge step.

My father got wind of the first letter and the second. He said in a stern voice, "He's pressuring you. He's older than you and in a different place in life. Plus, he's poor. What would you live on? Is that the life you want to have?"

"But Dad."

"End it with him and finish high school. Don't make a rash choice you'll regret later on."

I sent Harry a letter breaking up with him, but he showed up at our front door one afternoon a week later, looking pale and thin. I stood behind the screen door and didn't invite him in. He put his hands together, blue eyes staring, and said in a trembling voice, "I hitchhiked to get here. Please, reconsider. You're making a mistake, and we belong together."

I shook my head. "I don't want to move and get married. I'm sorry, but it's over."

"But we got along so well. It'd work. We'd have a good life."

My father appeared behind me, clearing his throat. "You'd better go."

Harry stared, his hands fidgeting at his side. "Can I at least get a glass of water and use the bathroom?"

My father said, "No, go home. That's all we have to say."

Harry looked down and sighed. He turned away, his thin shirt and jeans looking more worn and threadbare than usual, and he trudged away.

My father closed the door and frowned. "He needs a decent shirt and pants."

"But he's poor," I said. "He can't help it."

"I was poor once too. He should at least wear a clean shirt."

About a year later, my high school friends and I attended a talk given by a man from Harry's town, and I went up to him after the crowd thinned. "Do you happen to know Harry by chance?"

He furrowed his brow and studied me. "Yes, I know him. You must be the one who left him."

I winced. "Is he doing okay?"

"Last I saw him, he was standing by the side of the road in the rain with his redheaded girlfriend, and I gave them a ride."

I'd like to talk with my father and hear his thoughts about what happened when Harry came to our house, but

my dad died, and our shared memories are dust. One day
that summer, Harry bent over to kiss me by the river just
as my parents puttered past on their sailboat. My dad
turned his head and gaped. In my mind, Harry will be
forever about to kiss me by the river. But he's also standing
in the rain with his redheaded girlfriend, and I'm the
cruel one who wouldn't open the screen door to give him
water.

7

RETORT

Three days after my father passed away, I came upon information about his pacemaker's model number and manufacturer. I was about to throw it away, but my mother happened to see it and said, "Maybe someone else can use it."

I called the funeral home, where my dad was about to be cremated, and told them my father had a pacemaker. "My mother thought maybe someone else could use it."

A woman on the other end of the line said, "We didn't have that information. It was left off the intake form for some reason." She took down the details about the pacemaker's model and serial number and said, "If we hadn't caught that in time, our brand-new state of the art expensive retort would've blown up, and that wouldn't have been good."

I hung up and told my mother the news. Given my dad's history of making medical equipment malfunction in his later years, his body blowing up the retort would have been a fitting, unfortunate ending.

8

KIDNEYS

The ultrasound technician moved a wand over my pregnant belly, and I watched the display screen, frowning. I wasn't an expert, but it looked like she was focusing on my kidneys. There were definitely two of them.

She finished moving the ultrasound and stood, turning the display screen away from me and tapping on a keyboard. I covered myself with crinkling blue paper, and my husband, who had taken time off work for the ultrasound, leaned against the wall with his arms crossed. His brown eyes rested on mine, and he smiled.

The technician said, "Have you had an ultrasound before during this pregnancy?"

I shook my head. "No, this is the first one."

She tapped away, and I craned my neck to see the screen, where she was still looking at my kidneys. She glanced at my husband. "You may want to sit down for this."

He shrugged and flashed a smile. "I'm fine."

I bit my lower lip, worrying about what she might say. Was something wrong with our baby?

She looked at us. "Are you aware you're having twins?

My pulse raced, and a wide smile spread across my face. I beamed at my husband, and he grinned. He said, "Two of them?"

The technician smiled. "Yes."

We thanked her and left, walking hand in hand toward our doubly blessed future.

My son was visiting and we walked to the top of a viewpoint overlooking Cap Sante Marina and the town of Anacortes. We were taking in the view when a woman behind us said in a quiet voice, "Fire in the hole."

I whipped my head around and saw a man and woman in their late seventies standing by a cannon on wheels. The mouth of the cannon was aimed at us. I said, "What are you doing?"

The older grizzled man said, "Watch out, we're going to light it."

His co-conspirator, who appeared to be his wife with a matching age and size, said in a matter-of-fact voice, "Step aside."

My son and I looked at each other with raised eyebrows and moved away. Buddy, our beagle-mix rescue dog, wasn't happy, because he'd been sniffing a special spot at the top.

The couple didn't call out a warning to others. They lit the fuse. BOOM! BAM! The cannon went off, and the ground shook beneath my feet.

My dog yipped, I flinched, and we hoofed it down the hill as if pursued by an angry mob. A week later, I heard the cannon go off by the marina. It seemed the hobby of the cannon enthusiasts required frequent firings, at festivals, at the viewpoint and at the marina on Fridays at five o'clock.

Walking my dog, I took to taking furtive glances around corners and behind my back, especially if I was relaxed at a particularly beautiful spot. They were lurking in the park, at the top of the viewpoint, ready to fire into my son's back at any moment.

Finally, I spoke with a neighbor who was a veteran, and he said the sudden cannon explosions rattled him, reminding him of serving in the war. I mentioned I was jolted by the cannon blasts in town and suggested he tell someone down at city hall, because we probably weren't the only ones traumatized by the Friday five o'clock cannon firings. Sometime after that, silence became our friend, and only the sound of the breeze could be heard on Fridays at five in the afternoon.

10

NEEDLE

"Baby B has the needle," a man said. "Stop. Don't do anything."

My pulse quickened. Moments before, my twins had been swimming around in my womb, and a doctor slowly inserted an amniocentesis needle. My son grabbed it and held on.

"I've never seen this before. This is a first."

I tried to calm my racing heart. Something about the procedure was making me feel nervous, and my hands were sweaty. The length of the needle was a big part of the problem. It was so long, it looked like it could stretch all the way to the moon.

"Okay, Baby B let go. We can proceed."

Doctors recommended the test, and in the end, nothing alarming was revealed, except that I hate the sight of really long needles piercing my flesh. My son grew up with a love of sticks, and he picked them up at the beach, on walks and wherever he went. Perhaps that behavior started in the womb, or maybe not.

11

TOILET PAPER ROLL

I sat in the teachers' lounge sketching on my lunch break, where I worked in a high school library as an aide. I recommended *On the Road* to students to read, and our copies were soon stolen. We bought more, to encourage reading.

A man in his forties who worked at the school tapped a finger on the table, while I continued to draw. He said, "There's only one way to put a roll of toilet paper on the holder."

I glanced up from my colored pencil sketch. "What do you mean?"

He held up his hands. "Everyone knows this. It shouldn't be a point of discussion, but it was with my ex-wife. You put it on the holder so paper goes down the back."

I wrinkled my brow. "That's not how I do it. It comes out in the front."

He shook his head, jabbing a finger at me. "No way. People shouldn't do that."

"Sounds like there are a few ways to do it."

He stood. "Well, there shouldn't be. That was part of the reason we got divorced, plus that time she held a knife over my head while I was sleeping. I woke up in the night, saw the sharp blade in her hand and that did it."

I winced. "That'd do it for me."

He cocked his head and pointed to my abstract sketch. "Why do you do that anyways?"

"Do what?"

"Scribble on those pages with pencils."

I shrugged. "It feels good to draw. It's something I love to do."

He mumbled, "Whatever," and left the teachers' lounge.

I shook my head, knowing we were worlds apart and would remain that way, and went back to drawing.

12

UNIVERSITY DISTRICT STREET FAIR

I was five months pregnant and taking a nap on a vacant band platform at the University District Street Fair in Seattle. Fatigue washed over me, and I left my husband in charge of my booth. The car was parked too far away to walk to it for a short nap. I set my water bottle down and dozed off.

Voices close to me woke me. A man said, "What's in her water bottle? Tequila?"

A few guys laughed. I kept my eyes closed and hoped they'd move on to some other target. The first one said, "Let's piss on her."

I sat up and glared. "I'm pregnant. Leave me alone. I'm working the fair and taking a break."

Two guys in their late teens jeered at me, pointing and laughing. A young women wearing dark eyeliner, a black leather jacket and a short black shirt tugged on the leader's elbow. "Come on, let's go."

He yanked his arm away and stared at me, like I was a target for misplaced anger. I stood and clenched my fists, brandishing my water bottle as a weapon. This fair was notoriously crowded, where lanes were clogged with people, but I'd managed to find an out of the way spot, which I now regretted. My gaze flicked over the almost empty parking lot. The nearest person, other than these hoodlums, was fifteen yards away.

The leader glared and took a step toward me.

I said in my most threatening voice, "No one bothers a pregnant woman. What's wrong with you?" I pointed to the street. "Go on, get out of here, or I'll call the cops and report you."

"Come on," Ms. Leather Jacket said, pulling at his hand.

He gave me one last sneer and strode away. Motioning to his friends, he said, "Let's go."

I stood there trembling, watching them leave the parking lot. The smell of fried food hung heavy in the air. I sucked in a deep breath, patted my belly and went the other way back to my booth. I never saw those creeps again, and I hope now that they're older, if they're even still alive, they feel ashamed of themselves every time that memory flashes through their minds, which it should, but it probably doesn't. I enjoy studying human behavior and writing about weird people, but I can't fathom why they were acting aggressive and verbally abusive to a sleeping woman. Maybe they'll wake up one day, realize how vile they were and experience scorching self-retribution and burning shame.

13

SOCIAL STUDIES

I don't know what possessed me, but I wrote a note to my friend in seventh grade Social Studies class and folded it up, passing it to her through people from several seats back.

Mr. McMillan, who had the broad-shouldered build of a football player, stopped lecturing and walked over to my friend, taking the note from her hand. "I'll take that."

My friend turned in her seat and gaped at me. My body flushed with heat.

Our teacher said, "The punishment for passing notes in class and not paying attention is for me to read the note aloud."

My cheeks heated hot enough to fire a pottery kiln. I had a forest fire blazing inside. My armpits pricked with sweat. I wiped my sweaty upper lip.

Mr. McMillan unfolded the note, read it to himself

and gazed at me. Looking over the class, he said, "Here's what it says. And remember not to do this again unless you want everyone in class to hear it."

Holding the dreaded note higher in the air, he read in a high-pitched voice, "I have the biggest crush on Xavier. I love his sexy low voice."

Everyone laughed and turned to look at me, whispering behind their hands. I stared at the floor, studying scuff marks. My face was a furnace. I had to get out of here. Finally, the bell rang, signaling the end of class.

Out in the hall, Xavier, my crush and a trumpet player in the band, brushed past. I looked up at him hoping he'd be delighted to hear I was interested in him. But he snarled at me and said one word. "Slut."

I gasped and hurried to the bathroom, hiding there a long time. I wasn't sure what the word meant, but it sounded mean. I looked it up in our dictionary at home, but didn't find it, so it took a while for me to figure out what he meant.

I'm not sure why he said that to a red-faced, mortified girl standing in the hall filled with hope, and my only guess is he was harboring hidden simmering resentment from something that happened two years earlier. A carnival came to town when we were in fifth grade, and a boy who played French horn asked me to go with him. I would have preferred to go to the carnival with Xavier, but he didn't ask me. Back then, in the 1960's, girls didn't ask boys out, and only boys could be "Safety Boys," acting as volunteer crossing guards before and after school.

I went on the Ferris wheel and other rides with the French horn player, who asked me to go steady. I said yes, excited more by the daring idea than what it might mean, and he gave me a metal ID bracelet to wear, which I hid at home under the base of a lamp. My parents had no idea of the turbulence tearing through their daughter's life.

14

WATERING CAN

I carried an urgent document to the chief executive officer's corner office. My boss, head of corporate communications and investor relations, told me to place the important papers on the executive's chair, so he'd see them right away.

But as I approached the office, I noticed a man in his early thirties standing at the desk by an empty executive chair, reading papers left there. He wore a green apron, and in his right hand, he held a watering can.

I said, "Hello?"

He jerked around, looked at me, and strode over to a potted plant in a corner, watering it for a few seconds. He walked out, with his head turned away from me.

I set the documents down and told my boss what had happened. Security looked into the incident and discovered a high-powered telescope in a hotel room across the street was trained on our top executive's desk. They couldn't pin down who rented the room and set up the telescope, but we had a case of corporate espionage on our hands. Rumors flew about a possible merger, and many months later, the company was bought out. As far as I know, no one found out who was watching the chief executive's desk in the corner office and reading documents from across the street. Was the guy with the watering can aligned with the telescope spies or was he a separate sleuth? We'll never know, which is why I write mysteries and thrillers, to explore questions like that and offer answers in fictional worlds.

15

WHAT INSTRUMENT DO YOU PLAY

A birthday party for a percussion player was in full swing on my trumpet playing boyfriend's back deck. Two trombone players were mixing up special margaritas. They ran out of ice, and I hurried to a convenience store, lugging back cold bags. In the living room, a young woman was eating Twinkies from a stack on a serving platter, and Jerry's basset hound tipped over the glass coffee table in an attempt to consume liver pate.

I had just sat down on a porch swing out back, and the party swirled around me, when a tall man came over and said, "What instrument do you play?"

My eyebrows shot up. I was in my early forties, but I harkened back to my junior high days and said with a smile, "Flute."

He nodded. "That makes sense."

I later learned that woodwind players often match up

with brass players, like when I played flute in junior high and had a burning crush on a trumpet player.

A pregnant woman stood and diverted our attention, opening her jacket, pulling out an ultrasound and holding it in the air. As far as we knew, no one had invited her. She pointed at the ultrasound and announced the name of the father of her baby, but he wasn't there. A hush fell over the group before conversations resumed.

It was one of the strangest parties I've attended, due to Twinkies being offered as appetizers, the dog knocking over the bear coffee table and an ultrasound being waved around by a stranger. But the margaritas were delicious, and a good time was had by all. Except, later that night, after everyone left, I noticed a glass bowl on the dining room table near the front door had been stolen. We never found out who took it.

The porch swing I had given my boyfriend as a birthday gift finally wore out. The fabric split, but we didn't. We married, moved to a small town, and now we have a different dog and new patio swing. I wonder how a Twinkie would taste if it was dunked in liver pate for a weird snack. We almost found out that odd night.

Next up is Book 8, *Waterfall,* in the *Strangers on a Train Series*

WATERFALL

TRUE STRANGE TALES

1

LET ME SPEAK TO HIM

The landline at my folks' house rang, and I picked it up. I was screening calls for my mother, because my father had died two days before. "Hello?" I said.

"Let me speak to Edward," a woman said with a slight Southern accent.

I put a hand to my chest and couldn't speak, my mind filled with images of his last moments in bed and mortuary workers carrying out his body to an unmarked van.

She said in a gruff voice, "Let me speak to him. Now."

"No," I said in a choked voice.

"Where is he? Tell him I need to speak to him right now. Get him on the line."

"He isn't here," I said, gripping the phone tight, tears trickling down my cheeks.

"Where is he?" she barked. "This is social security calling."

"This is a cruel call. Do something different with your life."

I blocked the number, stared at dead flowers in the yard and let tears trickle down my cheeks, missing my father.

2

GRAY CAT

A strange gray cat has been attacking cats and dogs in our area, according to a neighbor. On a dog walk, I saw a gray cat in tall grass by a wetland, and I knocked on the neighbor's door to tell her. She came out and quickly shut the door, saying she didn't want her cat to see us.

I said, "Is the cat causing trouble a gray tabby or solid gray?"

She glanced toward her house, as if worried her cat might see her near my dog in what would be the ultimate betrayal. "Solid gray with white mittens and a kinked tail."

I walked away and called Animal Control, but they were closed until morning. Calling a police non-emergency line, the operator was blasé about our neighborhood kerfuffle. "Call Animal Control," he said.

"I did, but they're closed, and it's too bad, because we

know the whereabouts of the cat in question who is feral and attacking other animals."

He said in a slightly bored voice, "Call animal control when they open."

We hung up, and I walked home with my dog. Along the way, we saw the solid gray cat hiding in tall grass by the wet land. But to confuse matters, the dog and I noticed two other cats near the wetland. The black cat couldn't be the one causing problems. But the gray tabby has a kinked tail.

The neighbor's investigation continues into the culprit making deep scratches on dogs and cats, leading to costly vet bills. Life in a small town means everything, no matter how small, is of interest to everyone. My dog volunteered to catch the gray cat, but I told her our neighbor was handling it.

3

SHUSHING

I was creating an ad for one of my books, *Secrets at the Café*, and wanted to type the word 'mystery,' but what came out was 'shushing.' When I tried again, gibberish emerged on the document. Looking at the laptop's keyboard, I realized with horror that I couldn't recognize any of the letters.

I cocked my head, assessing the situation. My brain felt normal, except for a band of cold around my head. I could think, but something was definitely wrong.

My husband snored in the next room, napping in the late afternoon. I didn't want to wake him and hoped this episode signaled nothing big. I'd been sitting hunched over, so I stood and inhaled several deep breaths before searching for my phone. I couldn't remember my doctor's name, and it took me awhile to find it. My local doctor's office is owned by my health insurance company, which is strange, and when I called, a woman in a call center directed me to the walk-in clinic, but she said it was full and closing soon.

I hung up and felt light-headed and slow-minded. Any decision was too big a task.

My husband came in the kitchen, where I sat on a bar stool at the counter. "What's going on?"

"I couldn't make sense of letters on the keyboard, and I think something's wrong. The word mystery came out as shushing. They told me to go to the walk-in clinic."

He raised his eyebrows. "Forget the walk-in clinic. We're going to the ER."

But at the Emergency Room, where they got me in right away, something about an organ transplant was going on, and I didn't see the doctor on duty for five hours. Later, I examined the insurance company's statement and saw they refused to reimburse our local hospital for my ER visit because it took too long to see me.

Anyway, what I learned was, and I wanted to share this in case it helps you or a loved one, if you suspect you're having a stroke, take two aspirin under the tongue (I knew to do that but forgot) and call 911. Emergency medical technicians will take you to a facility and their patients have priority, because they call ahead and make arrangements to get their patients in right away for evaluation and tests.

I spent the night in the hospital and was evaluated via Zoom by a hospitalist in another town at two in the morning. She kept squinting at the screen and saying the picture of me was too small, and the nurse by my bedside said the hospitalist had to do that on her end, but she didn't know how. That was odd, in the middle of the night.

The next day, I had many tests, and the consensus was I'd had a TIA or mini-stroke, and the clot had passed. We're keeping a watchful eye on a carotid artery that is partially blocked. I hope this doesn't happen to you, but if it does, call 911 and be well.

4

STOMACH

I took my dog Buddy, an older beagle-mix rescue dog, to see the neighbors down the street, and we chatted at a round kitchen table about wildlife in town and movies to watch. When I stood to leave, Delia, a woman with white hair in her early eighties, lifted her shirt and showed me her stomach.

"Feel my stomach," she said, exposing her skin. "I have a hernia. They're taking it out next week."

I cocked my head. Her skin was gray and lumpy, like something was wrong.

"Feel it," she said.

I kept my hands to myself. "We'd better get going. Take care."

Buddy leaned forward on his leash to sniff her skin. He gave me a sad, serious look, the same one he'd given me before I was diagnosed with breast cancer. He sat and gazed at Delia, staring as trying to communicate what he sensed, but she waved him away. "Go on now."

I said, "I hope the surgery goes well," and Buddy and I left for a walk.

Some beagles can detect cancer, and they're trained to sniff it out. My mother told me about a bunch of beagles in her area who were trained for that purpose, but when they were taken out in public and sniffed certain people in the town square, individuals asked why the beagles had singled them out. This created difficult conversations, and the beagle trainers stopped taking the expert cancer sniffers to public places.

A week later, Delia had hernia surgery, and it turned out she had inoperable cancer. Buddy knew and tried to tell us, but we didn't listen. She passed away soon after, with family by her side.

5

___

SALEM

I drove from Seattle to a juried art show in Salem, Oregon. I managed to pack my booth and sixteen boxes of pottery in my station wagon but had to stop along the way to add radiator fluid. I set up my booth in the park early in the morning.

Thunder rumbled in the distance, and dark clouds scudded across the sky. I shivered in my sweatshirt and skirt, thinking this would pass. Rain started to fall, and people pulled up the hoods of their jackets.

A storm hit, and rain slashed down, puddles growing on the grass. I glanced at my pottery and poured water from a bowl, but it was coming down in torrents, so I gave up.

Across the way, a young paper artist was sobbing, her long black hair sopping wet. Her beautiful handcrafted papier-Mache sculptures were melting with the moisture, turning into white puddles of pulp. Like me, she didn't have a canopy over her booth.

I was four and a half hours from home and didn't want to leave my booth to cower in my car. I had paid a hefty fee to participate in the show, and I wanted to stay on site and try to make some sales. But I was cold and wet, without rain gear. This was in the days before cell phones, so I sent my boyfriend (we'll call him Starlight, because we met on a night when the stars were out and meteor showers filled the sky) a mind message, saying to bring rain gear and come help me.

Rain drove down harder, the paper artist cried, her shoulders shuddering. My teeth chattered, and I pulled on a wool hat. Time slowed, and it was only ten in the morning. A few hardy souls came out despite the weather, laughing and talking, and I chatted it up and sold some bowls.

By early afternoon, we'd had two inches rain. Starlight showed up, grinning and handing me rubber boots, a rain coat and wool socks.

He said, "I felt I had to drive here and help you. It woke me up."

6

SURROGATE

A man about my age, thirty years old, approached me at a business lunch about the possibility of my doing a market research project for his organization. We agreed to meet and discuss it, and he wanted to meet at The Deluxe Tavern in Seattle, a restaurant and bar.

He was already there when I arrived, and I took a seat at the two-top, facing the window. It was four o'clock in the afternoon, and we ordered beer. I asked about the upcoming project, but he waved it off, eying me up and down.

"Let's talk about you first. Do you work out?"

I furrowed my brow and sipped beer. Fine, I thought, I'll answer a few questions, establish trust and then we'll discuss work. "I walk a lot, and I hiked up Mt. Si recently."

He beamed at me, as if I'd won an award. "That's great. How much do you drink?"

I shrugged. This was getting weird, but I'd play along. "Not much."

He nodded and adjusted his glasses. I studied his gold wedding band, because the vibe I was getting was that he was single. My mind screamed at me to walk out and forget the project. This was too strange. But curiosity kept me in my seat, sipping beer.

I tapped the table. "So, about the project you mentioned."

He cleared his throat. "Have you thought about getting pregnant?"

I gulped. "I don't know. Let's talk about work instead."

He blabbed for a bit about a project that never came to fruition, and we parted ways. I told a colleague about the odd encounter, and she said in a low voice, "He's going around talking to people, and you're not the first. He and his wife want to have a baby, and they're looking for a surrogate."

7

STREET CORNER IN PARIS

I was in Paris for three days and going to as many museums as I could in the short time I had before boarding a night train to Florence, Italy. I'd eaten croissants from cafes, seen the Mona Lisa, and gaped at brushstrokes in Monet's waterlilies paintings. I'd met with a friend of a friend for dinner and walked along the Seine, going into Notre Dame.

I strolled down a street, considering where to go next. Paris in November felt like Seattle, with damp, gray skies and cool temperatures. I was wearing a black leather jacket, dark jeans, a black turtleneck, leather boots, and a magenta beret.

I stopped at a street corner, waiting for the light to change, and a well-dressed man in a business suit came up to me, flashing a slow, alluring smile. He took off his black felt hat and held it to his chest.

Looking into my eyes, he said in a deep voice, "May I help you?"

I tilted my head, not sure what to say. "I'm fine."

He continued to gaze at me. "Would you like assistance of any kind?"

The light changed, and I understood finally what he was saying. "No, thanks."

I made my way across the street and glanced back when I reach the opposite side.

The man was still standing where I left him, hat against his heart, looking my way. I smiled and walked on, leaving him right where he'll always remain in my mind.

8

RAT

I listed my car for sale in the local paper, back before we had the internet.

A man called five times, using different accents, but from the same phone number. Each time he'd say something like, "It's too old. It's not worth that much." And he'd hang up.

I'd glance at caller ID and listen to him, rolling my eyes. His German accent was my favorite. I needed to sell the car because for a reason I can't recall, I hadn't traded the car in when I bought a new car with a loan payment I could afford.

The man called a last time, without an accent. "It's probably not worth much, but I'll take a look at it. Has anyone else called about it?"

"A few people called," I said with a shrug.

"Has anyone come by?"

"Not yet."

"Are you negotiable on price?"

I nodded. "I might be, but I replaced the transmission, the radiator, and the tires. It's in good shape."

We set up a meeting in front of my house, because I wasn't smart enough to meet him in a store parking lot away from home. He arrived, looked the car over and nodded. "Can you start the car?"

I got behind the wheel and turned the key. Stepping out, I watched him listen to the engine. He sniffed the air and made a face. "Something smells."

I inhaled but didn't detect anything out of the ordinary. I suspected he was making something up to negotiate a lower price.

He opened the hood and gasped. "That's why it stinks."

I bent over and stared at a dead black rat roasting on the engine block. I shook my head and figured the rat must have climbed in at the Park N Ride, when I parked by a bunch of blackberry bushes a few days before and took the bus to work. I waved a hand in front of my face and breathed through my mouth, trying to ignore the foul odor.

He let the hood fall down with a thump. "It's bad luck. I can't buy it now."

He started to leave, but his steps were slow.

"Wait," I called. "Come back, and let's talk."

That's how I sold a car with a surprise rat to a man who got a good deal.

9

BLAKELY ISLAND

I was going through chemotherapy and other treatments and experiencing brain fog, so much that I gave the wrong phone number and email address to a gallery owner who was selling my paintings. Jerry and I went out on our boat whenever we could, and I worked remotely on the Salish Sea. Smelling the briny sea air made me smile, and being on a boat, plowing through the water, brought back pleasant childhood memories.

Perhaps I was over confident the day I jumped down on the dock at Blakely Island. Or my mind was muddled and I didn't realize what was happening until too late. Jerry was at the helm, and I was in charge of tying our lines to the dock. The dog was supposed to stay on board, until we were ready to walk with the dog on leash to land. It is a mostly private island, and the marina has a small area to explore for dog walks.

I stepped on the dock and moved to a cleat with the stern line. We didn't realize it, but a strong current was pushing the boat away from the dock. I knew I needed to move faster, but I was stuck in molasses. I was too slow to get a good wrap of the stern line around a cleat. The stern started drifting away from the dock.

Our dog, a beagle-mix rescue dog Buddy, hopped off the boat and raced down the dock. I called for him to come, but he ran to land. I frowned, because landowners on the mostly private island wouldn't be pleased to see Buddy racing around on his own.

I turned my attention to the bow, just as Jerry jumped off the boat to help me. I felt like I was in a snow globe, where someone shook up what was normal and everything was upside down. It was all going wrong, and it was my fault.

Jerry and I watched the boat drift away from the dock. No one was at the helm. No one was on board. No boaters were around to help us. The marine radio and our cell phones were on the boat. We couldn't call for help.

Jerry had worked for the ballet, but not as a dancer who flew through the air. He was a trumpet player. But he extended his arms and pushed off from the dock, leaping over the water and clinging to the bow as the current carried it away. He hauled himself onboard the boat and hurried to the helm.

I pointed at the blue bow line that was in the water

and called to him, "The bow line is in the water. It could wrap around the prop."

He cupped a hand behind his ear. "What?"

I yelled, "The bow line. Pull in the bow line."

He shook his head. "I can't hear you." He put the boat in gear and a grinding sound came over the water. He put it in neutral and frowned. "Got a line around the prop."

"The bow line," I yelled pointing to the stern. "It's back there."

He stared at the back of the back, swore and went back in the wheelhouse, putting the engine in reverse for a short burst. Putting it in neutral, he came out and hauled the errant dock line onboard. "I got it out. I put it in reverse."

I cheered but glanced toward land, looking for our dog and not seeing him or a hint of his curly tail. Jerry still needed to dock, despite a strong current pushing the boat toward the channel, so I focused on being a better first mate. He brought the boat to the dock and kept her there using the bow thruster, while I scurried around tying lines the way I should have done the first time. If anyone was watching our circus act from a cabin on shore, they must have chuckled at our frantic antics.

When the boat was securely tied up, we walked down the dock, and I let out a long, loud whoosh of breath. Our dog came running toward us with a smile, acting as if everything was fine. Which it was, but it certainly hadn't been. After that, I invested in special headsets, so we could talk to each other while docking, saving us from making other maritime disasters.

10

JOB OFFER

I had arranged interviews with two international market research companies in Hong Kong and flew there, back when international calls were prohibitively expensive and business people communicated by telex international messages. I stayed at the YWCA, where you could rent a clean private room for a decent price, and walked on Victoria Peak, looking down on the harbor and the teeming city. I sipped steaming hot coffee mixed with sweetened condensed milk from a street vendor.

I entered a tall building and took the elevator up for the interview at the first company. In the position I was interviewing for, I'd be the account manager for ex-pat clients, mostly from the U.S. or Australia. When I met the director who would be my boss, he held my hand a bit too long, and his gaze flicked over my body, as if measuring me for clothes. I shrugged it off, thinking it was due to cultural differences.

He led me through the office, and a hush fell over the space. Workers at desks turned in swivel chairs, watching my every step. I smiled and waved and carried on, confident in my blue and white pinstriped two-piece skirted suit. The interview went well, and he offered me a job on the spot. The previous person in the position was an Aussie who had gone home, and they needed to fill the vacancy.

At the second company, I sat in a high-rise building with a view of the bustling city. A woman and a man, two Americans in their early thirties, asked questions about my background. Finally the woman, a brunette with an intense gaze, nodded to the man and told me they didn't have anything at the time, but they'd keep me in mind.

I said, "I understand. I think I'll take the offer the other company made."

Her eyebrows shot up, and she leaned forward, looking into my eyes. "Do you know what you'll have to do there?"

"Meet with clients, oversee market research surveys, prepare reports and make presentations."

She tilted her head. "And?"

"I think that's it."

She turned to the man. "She doesn't know."

He put a hand over his mouth and whispered, "We've got to tell her."

She swallowed. "You'll be expected to sleep with the director."

My eyebrows shot up. "Pardon me?"

They nodded. He said, "We thought we should warn you."

I tapped my chin, thinking how people's eyes travelled over my body as I walked through the first company, and corners of women's mouths turned up in knowing smiles. Saved from a naïve blunder, I blew out a breath. "Thank you for telling me."

I appreciate their honesty to this day.

11

BEIJING

I was asked by a man who owned an import-export business in Tacoma, Washington, who was on a sister-city trade mission with me to China, to deliver a package in Beijing.

The train chugged north for three days, and I had a sleeping compartment to myself. But on the third morning, a porter knocked and came in, making frantic gestures for me to get dressed and pack my things, which I did. The door soon swung open, and three men in business suits came in, sitting in silence until the train pulled into the station in Beijing.

I took a taxi to the ministry of agriculture and walked in the door. I asked to speak with someone in animal husbandry, or something like that, and was directed to a man at a desk. I introduced myself, handing him my Chinese-English business card.

I said, "I was asked to deliver this to your office." I handed a package to him, glad to have done my duty by dropping it off.

He hefted it in his hands. "What's in it?"

"Bull semen."

"What did you say?"

"It has bull semen in it. I'm told it is of high quality. There's information in the package about it."

He cocked his head and stared, perhaps wondering if this was a weird joke. But it wasn't. I left and made my way back in time to tour the Forbidden City. But my adventure to the Great Wall did not go as smoothly.

Two people had told me it was faster, easier and the same price to take a taxi to see the Great Wall, instead of going on a tour bus. A brunette at lunch waved her fork in the air, saying, "It's much better without all those tourists."

The hotel helped me hire a taxi to see the Great Wall, and the drive took longer than I expected. The driver stopped and frowned a few times, checking a map, and finally we turned up a steep dirt road. A few miles later, he stopped the car and pointed through trees to a wall, far off in the distance. "That is the Great Wall. Now we go back."

"But you said you'd take me there. I want to see it up close and walk on it."

He shook his head. "This is it. You've seen the Great Wall."

"Please, take me closer."

Eventually, he did, but I should have hopped on a tour

bus with other tourists. It would have been faster and cost less in the end. And I learned the importance of being precise. There is a huge difference between saying, "I want to *see* the Great Wall," and, "I want to go to the Great Wall." My mistake.

12

WATERFALL

I told my husband I'd always wanted to go to Lake Havasu, Arizona, so we flew into Los Angeles, rented an RV and drove there on vacation. But when I climbed out and looked at cigarette boats racing on the reservoir, I wrinkled my nose and said, "This isn't it. I meant Havasu Falls."

The man we'll call Starlight, because we met on a night when the sky was filled with stars and meteor showers, sighed, and we climbed in the RV and drove to the top of the Havasu Canyon. That night, after dark, someone pounded on the door. A man said in a loud voice, "We need trash bags."

My husband opened the door and handed a man on horseback trash bags. The paper bags with groceries had ripped. He said, "Thanks, if you're ever in the canyon, look me up. I'm Gary." He told us where his house was, and he and his horse clomped away in the dark, followed by two men on horseback.

The next day, we rose early and packed bottles of water and trail mix for the upcoming trek down to the bottom of the canyon. On the way down the ten-mile trail to Supai Village, the capital of the Havasupai Indian Reservation, a red-faced hiker walking up stumbled on the path.

"Do you have any water?" he said, wiping sweat from his brow. "Mine ran out."

I looked at Starlight and shrugged. We handed the man, who said he was from Germany, one of our bottles of water and continued hiking for four hours. It was hot but not horrendous, going downhill.

We came upon a rattlesnake, dead but coiled as if ready to strike. Horse's hooves marked the area, so perhaps the men on horseback had passed this way the night before. I squealed and jumped back from the venomous exposed fangs, but Starlight bent and picked up the rattlesnake, carrying it as we walked along.

"Let's go see him," Starlight said, and we walked toward the house the man on horseback had mentioned. Two muscled men in black t-shirts stood blocking the path. They stared at the rattlesnake and at Starlight. One said, "Who are you?"

"We're here to see Gary," Starlight said, indicating the

house. "We met him last night and gave him garbage bags. He invited us to stop by."

The two guards glanced at each other and shrugged, stepping aside. "Go ahead."

We tromped down the dirt trail and knocked on a door. The man we'd met opened the door and squinted at us in the sun.

"We met you last night," I said.

Starlight added, "You said to stop by."

Gary ran a hand through his hair, staring at the rattlesnake. "You gave me trash bags?"

"Yep." Starlight handed the snake to him, saying, "I brought this, if you want it."

Gary set it down. "I'll take you to a secret place no one else knows."

He took us to Havasu Falls, and we stared at the blue-green color. He told us there were problems with visitors ignoring posted signs saying "No nude sunbathing." He motioned for us to follow him, and we went down a side trail and came to a pool of water. He said, "Let's join hands and go in. Make a wish as you jump."

I made a wish, and we held hands, jumping into refreshing, cool water. Every nerve in my body was tingling and alive, and I grinned.

He pointed ahead. "Hold your breath, swim under and come up in a sacred pool."

I held my breath, and followed him, swimming underwater and coming out into a natural pool surrounded by rock. He invited us to spend the night in a tent in his yard. Horses clomped around the tent all night. Stars sparkled and a full moon illuminated a dirt path as I made my way to the outhouse. At some point before dawn, the front door to the house was flung open, and our host tossed the dead rattlesnake on the roof. His cat had been playing with it, we learned the next morning.

Thanks for reading this! Please let other readers know what to expect by posting ratings and reviews on Goodreads, Amazon and BookBub.

Please tell your friends about the *Strangers on a Train Series*. Thanks!

Sign up on my website www.susanspechtoram.com for my author newsletter to hear about new releases and bookish news.

Follow me on BookBub for updates: https://www.bookbub.com/authors/susan-specht-oram

Find me on my Facebook author page: Susan Specht Oram Author

My YouTube channel @susanspechtoramauthor shows author chats and nature photography.

ABOUT THE AUTHOR

Susan is writing mysteries-thrillers and creative nonfiction. Previously, she served as senior director of corporate communications for biotechnology companies. Susan worked as an activity aide in an upscale nursing home's secure psychiatric unit. She was a potter and painter with an art studio in Seattle and has also worked as a market researcher, a nurse's aide, a waitress, and a library page. Her essays have been published in Mothering Magazine, Twins Magazine and Utne Reader. Susan grew up near Detroit, Michigan. She lives in a windy part of the Pacific Northwest with her husband and rescue dog.

BOOKS BY SUSAN SPECHT ORAM

Shore Lodge

The Thieves

Cabin Eight

Secrets at the Café

The Mother's Threat

Under Jackson Bridge

Missing Man

By Midnight

The Winter Storm

The Cold Night

Avalanche (coming Fall 2025)

Strangers on a Train series:

Green Light

The Train

Canoe

Soup Kettle

Bathtub

Phone Call

Watering Can

Waterfall

Strangers on a Train (Books 1-8)

Humorous fiction:

Boating with Buddy, a report from a canine correspondent

Nonfiction:

Brief business books on investor relations, crisis
communication and public relations